Shipping Container Homes

A Hand Book of Shipping Container House Plans to Constructing an Eco-Friendly Home, Plus Design Ideas and Tips to Get You Started

By

Kelsey Bates

Copyright © 2021 – Kelsey Bates

All rights reserved

No part of this publication may be reproduced, distributed, or transmitted in any form or by any means, including photocopying, recording, or other electronic or mechanical methods, without the prior written permission of the publisher, except in the case of brief quotations embodied in reviews and certain other non-commercial uses permitted by copyright law.

Disclaimer

This publication is designed to provide competent and reliable information regarding the subject matter covered. However, the views expressed in this publication are those of the author alone, and should not be taken as expert instruction or professional advice. The reader is responsible for his or her own actions.

The author hereby disclaims any responsibility or liability whatsoever that is incurred from the use or application of the contents of this publication by the purchaser or reader. The purchaser or reader is hereby responsible for his or her own actions.

Table of Contents

Introduction 8

Chapter 1 10

The Basics of Shipping Container 10

    What is a Shipping Container Home? 10

    Brief History of Shipping Container Homes 12

    Challenges of Shipping Container Homes 14

    Benefits of Shipping Container Homes 19

Chapter 2 24

Shipping Containing Home Startup Tips 24

Chapter 3 32

Home Layout Plan 32

    Plan 1 32

    Plan 2 36

    Plan 3 40

    Plan 4 44

Plan 5 48

Plan 6 52

Chapter 4 53

Selecting The Right Container 53

    Importance of Container Condition 54

    Right Time to Inspect a Container 55

    What to Inspect and How? 57

    Documentation 61

    Conditions and Container Grades 62

    Why Choose New (and New-ish) Containers? 67

    Why Choose Used Containers? 68

    Cost of Shipping Containers 69

    Shipping Container Condition to Buy? 70

    Buying Your Containers 71

    Choosing a Container Dealer 75

Chapter 5 80

Preparation of Site and Foundation 80

   Preparation of Site 80

      Choosing Your Location 80
      Site Work 84
   Foundation 87

      Is Foundation Necessary for Containers? 87
      Foundation Types for Containers 88
      Strength of Foundation Concrete to Use 90
      How to Attach Containers to Foundations 91

Chapter 6 93

Container Insulation 93

   What is Insulation? 93

   Reason to Insulate Your Container? 94

   The Effect of Climate on Your Choice of Insulation 94

   How to Place Your Container Insulation 95

   Choosing Your Insulation 96

   Types of Insulation for Containers 97

Chapter 7 103

Container Movement and Delivery 103

   Moving a Shipping Container Across Your Property 103

   Moving a Shipping Container Across Your City 104

Moving a Shipping Container Across Your State or Country 105

Moving a Shipping Container Across The World 107

Preparing a Container For Movement 107

Loading and Offloading Your Shipping Containers 109

Chapter 8 117

Installation of Utilities 117

    Electricity 117

    Gas 119

    Sewer and Septic 119

    Telecommunication 120

    Water 120

Chapter 9 123

Roofing The Container 123

Chapter 10 128

Container Flooring 128

Chapter 11 135

Constructing A Wall Inside The Container 135

Chapter 12 141

Door and Window Installation 141

Chapter 13 151

Finalizing The Exterior 151

Chapter 14 167

Ideas for Your Interior Design 167

    Design Idea 1 168

    Design Idea 2 170

    Design Idea 3 173

    Design Idea 4 176

Chapter 15 181

Shipping Container Home Mistakes to Avoid 181

Chapter 16 188

Shipping Container Home FAQs 188

Conclusion 195

Introduction

Since the invention of shipping containers, companies and business persons have gotten exposed to the possibility of shipping very heavy goods from one part of the world to another. Commerce has been made easy and faster. Many persons have access to products their country cannot produce. Thanks to the existence of shipping containers, centralization and decentralization of the economy can now be made easier. People from different parts of the world can easily transport basic materials or substances from one point to the other. However, this doesn't mean that shipping containers are infallible. Just like every invention, they have certain limitations and shortfalls, which could be quite challenging. Thanks to researchers who have taken their time to study and reveal possible and easy ways of handling a shipping container. One of the discovered ways of handling shipping containers is by converting them to shipping container homes. This is a new innovation that is becoming a trend.

There are limitless designs and models of shipping containers that can be created for various functions. Shipping containers can be used in modeling any structure. It has been proven to be a better and more bio-gradable way of building than the conventional traditional setup. The shipping containers are lesser expensive ways of building modern structures, it is also durable and mostly adopted because of its flexibility. Setting up a container home is not as technical as it sounds. The container already has the box shape of a conventional home, all you have to do is modify it into the structure you want. The beauty of your container home is dependent on the quality and design structure of your container home. In this book, we will be looking at how to turn a plain shipping container home into a building structure that you will love.

Chapter 1

The Basics of Shipping Container

What is a Shipping Container Home?

Several building structures/types fall under shipping container homes. In well-developed countries, container architecture is a trending business. Container construction is such a fascinating and unending creative building option that several architectures and individuals have to fall in love with.

It is a challenge to assess or reveal innovation and creativity. There are several types of container cabins; single-unit containers, tiny houses on the wheels, huge family homes built with the support of adjacent walls. There are first-class hybrid buildings that can be created with shipping containers. In certain situations, the hybrid buildings must blend with the traditional construction. One of these methods includes establishing traditional buildings on the top of containers, buildings with containers inside, or containers jutting out from the side.

There are modern decoration styles with exterior and interior modifications that make it impossible for you to tell whether it is really a container building except you were present at the construction. There are very interesting and almost unbelievable structures of container buildings. In some cases, they are assembled in large, organized rectangular forms, they are sometimes stacked, twisted, and turned in a way that makes them exciting to behold.

They are very flexible building alternatives as they can be modified to fit into any shape or building structure. In another sense, there is no limit to what you can do with the shipping container. The relevance of shipping containers cannot be judged from the size, their appearance, or the rate of their usage. Containers are majorly described by the structures it is used to build. There are popular assumptions that containers involve a narrow view of the available architectural concepts. There is also the assumption that shipping container homes are small and comes in metal exterior. Hence, so many are aversive to the shipping container idea.

Statistics have it that in time to come, shipping container homes will become a broad term with an endless availability of various designs.

Brief History of Shipping Container Homes

An amazing and almost unbelievable study reveals that there was nothing like shipping containers a few decades ago. Which is a total reverse of today's situation. A large percentage of the world economy is assisted and facilitated by the existence of shipping containers. One would wonder what was the former pillar holding the world economy in place before now. Well, all thanks to the ingenious individuals who took the pain to bring about this innovation that has indeed made the world a better place.

Basically, containers started as a means of transporting goods from a place to another. Today, containers are being modified for building houses for people. These housing containers have turned out to be a hot architectural cake for all types of projects. More modifications of container houses keep evolving such that you can build a container house and place it anywhere for commercial or family use. Let's take a little slide back to the beginning of all the modifications.

The container was invented out of the desire to solve the problem of commuting goods on land or sea to various locations and ensuring that they arrive safely. Although goods were being transported before the invention of containers, the methods were unsafe and inefficient.

Here is a brief list of the motivation behind the invention of shipping containers;

- They had a large capacity to contain goods of large mass, but could also fit into small trucks and drive normally.
- It has a very solid frame that protects its content in case of accidental clashes on land and sea.
- It is highly protective and easily moveable.
- The container is well flexible and allows for the movement of different sizes of goods from location to location.

One of the most popular brains behind this invention is the celebrated Malcolm McLean. He was driven by the desire to improve the economic level around the world, the shipping container seems to be a perfect solution. Another solid thing this invention did was that it helped to establish a level of standardization in the business world.

However, before 1980, there were more than enough shipping containers that were not in use. It was all turning into abuse before certain explorers started to experiment with the transformation of these dormant containers into habitable places. This was how the design and structuring of shipping containers for building started.

Challenges of Shipping Container Homes

Objectivity is a precious virtue when discussing any subject matter as it gives you a full perception of the situation. Giving you the view of the positive and negative at the same time, hereby allowing you to fully understand the nature of the decision you intend to make. If you will be considering owning a shipping container home, you must get to understand that there are possible limitations and challenges you might encounter. Some of them are surmountable if you know the tricks and where to pull the strings. Sometimes, you might still find it difficult to understand how to go about pulling these tricks. This is what makes the challenges insurmountable. A few of the challenges are listed below;

1. Room widths: shipping containers are known to come in a variety of heights and lengths, however, they only come in one width. In the united states, all containers are measured at 8 feet wide, irrespective of their size. This could be

quite limiting, especially when you put in interior walls, insulations, and other materials, the room becomes smaller and gets reduced to 7 feet. You might not understand this trouble except you have had the chance of spending time in a container building. Section 304 of the IRC states that habitable rooms must have a floor width of at least 7 feet. Even if your area doesn't use this code, the fact remains that a good living space should have space for many reasons which border on the livability, health, and safety of the inhabitants. This could be a very serious issue if you're just moving from a large house or you have a large family size. However, attempts have been made to solve this problem by placing containers beside each other and cutting through them to make them wider than normal. You can widen your space depending on the number of containers you have available for use. You can also use the parallel space between two containers with natural building materials, and using the inside of the containers for bathrooms, kitchens, and other required space. This shows that the challenge of space can actually be overcome if well construed. With the right construction strategies and some extra funds, you can scale through this challenge.

2. Insulation location: the corrugated metal sheets in shipping containers are a very important part of the structure that makes it unique. As aesthetic as this looks, it poses a serious challenge when you want to place insulation. Unlike the traditional building construction that allows you to break open the wall or bore holes into the wood with studs, it is almost impossible to create a cavity inside the container for imputing insulation. In solving this problem, some architects place insulation inside or outside the container. Whichever you choose, what is important is that you cover the insulation at the end. If you put it inside, you'd need to spend some more money in using aesthetic coverings to modify it. This also means that you would have little space in the container. If this insulation is placed outside the container, you would have to secure aesthetic and protective coverings to protect it from harsh weather conditions. All of the options are good enough depending on your budget and which

you consider best. Note that your decision is affected by nature and in turn, it affects every other thing from temperature to utility bills, and humidity.
3. Building code confusion: building codes vary based on the location of the occupants. There is a more serious problem in interpreting codes. Your structure could be construed by an individual or a location code. Although, no location outrightly forbids the building or setting up of a container home. Hence, you might need to just take some extra time and make modifications to your designs to suit the location code. You can learn and discover the means of administering rules for shipping container homes. This way you will find it easier to legally build your container home. A Panadol for your headache, consult a professional before you set out.
4. Safety and health concerns: this is one major concern when constructing a building or housing location. This is an issue that comes with small space. Several possible health and safety issues could come up in the container like pest invasion, paint leads, lighting electrocution, and others.

There are certain building materials like wood and paints when used in a container that could pose a challenge to the health of its occupant. Pests invasion from wood, chemicals from paints, and others. However, there are abatements methods to reduce the existence of these chemicals and paints. Most of them are costly and require serious labor. It is best to get a professional to abate these issues.

5. Controversial appearance: it is a sad truth that people still fail to appreciate the benefits and value of container homes. This is a result of ignorance and less publicity on the amazing container homes. Another contributory issue is that humans' preferences are wide and cannot be streamlined or categorized. Everyone has their likes and dislikes; no structural standard can be established based on likes. Wrong perceptions could be a serious issue in getting people to accept the ingenuity of container homes. If you want to own a container home, you might need to enlighten people around on the qualities of container homes.

6. Locating experienced contractors: even if you are well knowledgeable on how to build a container home from start to finish, you still need the services of an experienced contractor, because if you have the skill, you might not have the time to commit to the rigorous building process. Before hiring a contractor, you have to find out his level of experience and determine your level of involvement. If you want to have zero involvement, then you should be on the lookout for contractors that have long-term experience in building container homes.

Benefits of Shipping Container Homes

There are inexhaustive benefits of a shipping container home. However, these benefits are well in sight when used in the right situation, for the right individuals and for the right purpose. So, before you consider a shipping container home for a certain purpose, you have to check if it fits your personal objective and budget. Don't allow yourself to get distracted by the large number of incredible designs out there. This is why you need to have a preference list that will guide your selection decision.

1. Affordability: shipping containers are not the most affordable housing option available, depending on the size and type of container you get, it can prove to be a really cost-effective option for constructing a building. The major factors that influence container cost include style or design, size, and required labor on construction. There are very major advantages containers have over the traditional construction option especially if you do them in the right way and with the right experts. The main trick is to accept containers the way they are and use them the way they are for a fitting purpose than taking the laborers to work on them to modify them for another purpose. Read about the designs of the containers you are considering before you order them. A more practical way to save money is to review your options and select with practical and applicable expectations.
2. Sustainability: alternatives that offer recyclable options are considered sustainable in every field. Recyclables aid to improve waste management as they convert non-decomposable waste for reusability. Shipping container allows you to

reuse metal wastes for more healthy and effective purposes. That is, containers that are ineffective for carrying goods can be used in building comfortable and aesthetic habitable buildings. Also, they help reduce the tons of waste produced from the traditional construction process. It is a neater and healthier way of building. Shipping containers can be said to be environmentally friendly.

3. Strength and stability: metals are generally strong materials, so you can trust that shipping containers are stable and strong because they are made with metals. You can comfortably use them to ship goods and materials across oceans and large seas. Metals are also known to withstand pressure, weight and wears. They are also known for their sharp durability. If you are concerned with building a solid, strong and durable structure that can last for a long time, the shipping container is a very viable option for you to take advantage of. It is your sure bet to withstand toughness, and guarantee longevity.

4. Unique: most shipping containers look alike and have the same model and size. It is sometimes

difficult to identify the uniqueness in each of these individual container. The uniqueness of containers is not necessarily the style or size, it is the bracket of possibilities available to you. In another sense, the uniqueness lies in what you can do with the material.

It may look impossible to modify a plain simple item into a unique house or building. There are several ways to modify, combine and utilize shipping containers.

5. Flexibility: this feature or advantage is contributory to the uniqueness of shipping containers. Containers have a different level of flexibility. This is what makes them generally outstanding. You can move them easily through all the mediums of transportation; sea, road, rail. You can transport these containers through different vehicles on these mediums. Your container could also fit into any factory, building, or land space. You could also use the container for construction projects spreading over months. However, do not place your focus only on the location of your container home. You should also

be mindful of the structure you intend to put up that will suit your location. Generally, people are appealed by homes they can naturally set up themselves, and shipping containers are location flexible. You can set them up anywhere. It also offers flexibility options after construction. You can build down and build up again in a fair period of time.

Chapter 2

Shipping Containing Home Startup Tips

With the thousands of shipping containers lying useless at sea ports or factories, you would wonder if indeed there is a value or importance attached to these pieces of metals. All of these containers actually have the right size for a home. All it requires is for you to acquire these containers and stack them or line them side by side, your house is ready. But this is not all of it. Theoretically, building a shipping container home appears straightforward. You would put yourself under a whole lot of stress if you start off with this orientation.

There are several things you need to note to ensure that your container home has a sound structure and is aesthetically attractive. Twelve tips have been constructively included in this chapter to educate you on the steps to take to ensure that you get your container home off the ground on a good note. They are listed below;

1. See before you buy: this is simply a rational counsel. You would not buy anything you intend

to use for very cogent purposes without feeding your eyes on them, especially when it is a used product. Many persons get relaxed when buying a shipping container with the notion that they are all the same sheets and folds of metals. As much as this is true in a sense, a used shipping container could be in a fairly bad state that makes it unfit for building a container home. Some of them come with rusts, structural defaults, and many other dents. These dents are most common with containers that have lasted a long while. Brand new containers might be too expensive for you to get, so if you are settling for a used container, ask the sellers for detailed pictures and a total description of the container before making the purchase. You might be lucky enough to find a really good one with strong structures, and save yourself the stress and money of fixing a dented container.

2. Knowing your building code restrictions: several towns and cities have stipulated restrictions regarding building a shipping container home. Before making the purchase, and investing your thousands of dollars check your local building

codes. It is important to acquaint yourself with these restrictions before designing your building structure. These restrictions can affect your location choice, design choice, and quantity of permittable containers on a zone. However, don't let this be a turn-off for you, certain developed cities have favorable regulations for shipping container homes.
3. Make sure you have a plan for insulating: if you fail to insulate your container home properly, you are bound to have unbearable heat conditions during summer and unbearable freezing conditions during winter. In your structural design, make sure to make a detailed plan for insulating your container wall and roofs fully. Insulation options range from blanket-style to foam insulation, to sheep wool or green wool. All these options require different insulation methods and implications. Look out for the one that suits you best.
4. Find a complete contractor: building a shipping container home on your own is practically impossible except you have experience in contraction. Knowing is not enough, you can

make a total disaster if you decide to build your container home based on your knowledge. Ensure to get a contractor to oversee the whole building process right from your purchasing decision stage. It might be difficult to get shipping container contractors, but it is worth every stress it requires because having a contractor saves you a lot of stress and money. However, you will still have to budget for the contractor's pay.

5. Protect against harmful chemicals: note that shipping containers were designed with the vision of having them for a lifetime at the sea, hence taking them as a building alternative requires certain consciousness and extra structuring. First of all, the wood on the floor needs to be heavily treated with pesticides to dissuade the invasion of pests and rodents from biting through the woods. Also, the paints contain chemicals that help to reduce the effect of saltwater spray used on the containers when they were at the port. Foam insulations also help to reduce the effect of these chemicals which poses dangers to the human health.

6. Avoid cutting your containers into pieces: shipping containers are built with one of the strongest types of steel there is, it can bear several tons of load. However, whenever you cut an opening on your container, probably for a window or door, you are weakening the structural stability of your container. To reduce this effect, you'll need to acquire a steel beam reinforcement. The more cuts you make, the more reinforcements you'll need to gather, the more money you'll add to your budget.
7. Plan for plumbing and electrical: this is very necessary when structuring your design. Determine where you are going to have the plumbing and electrical materials fixed in your building and how you want it to be fixed. Make sure that these places are cut open and prepared before you finish your work on the interior of the container. This will guarantee that your house is in perfect shape and you won't need to undo any finishing.
8. Know the differences between containers: permit me to use this tip as a strong wield to finally debunk the understanding that all containers are

the same. Not all containers have the same structure, length, and height. The only common thing containers share in different districts or locations is width. Hence, you need the consider these other differences when purchasing your container. If you buy an averagely tall container, you will have a very uncomfortable space left after insulation.

9. Prepare for the wind: building a container home in a windy area could be quite discomforting because of the produced noises when the wind comes in contact with your container. Containers are more disposed or likely to be affected by winds because of their rectangular and metallic structure. You can reduce this effect by building your container home behind any structure that can withstand the wind and prevent it from having direct contact with your container.

10. Avoid excessive welding to cut costs: building a container home requires a lot of aesthetic costs that could keep your budget sheet pretty long, hence you should consciously be on the lookout for alternatives that would help to reduce these costs and minimize your budget. When designing

your structure avoid making aesthetics or designs that will require extra welding. Sometimes it could be pretty hard to do so, especially if you intend to make a story or two-story buildings or expand your container space by adding several containers together. However, you can still be strategic enough to know how to limit the required welding in other to take away that extra cost.

11. Consider local and vernacular options first: shipping containers are incredibly unique housing options because of their flexibility and sustainability. However, you can start off by considering already existing options. Instead of going as far as the sea port which could be as far as several miles away from your house just to get a shipping container for building, you can acquire a container from any vendor or factory close to your location. Also, you can consider using traditional construction methods in establishing and setting up your container home. You can include structural designs like natural plasters, bales, and bricks.

12. Be willing to spend the extra dollar: several persons who ever considered building a container home expect that they will be able to own their own house with little money, however, this expectation can be misplaced. In as much as shipping containers are very much affordable and relatively easy to build, designing the interior and exterior of a shipping container can increase your required expenditure. Also, note that the large and complicated the structure, the more costly it will be. The cost of fixing up the interior and exterior of a complicated container home design might be equal the cost of acquiring a traditional mortar and brick home.

Chapter 3

Home Layout Plan

A shipping container is a great building option because just like a drawing board, you can express your creative imaginations. It is incredibly amazing that just after you make careful consideration and provision for storage spaces, aesthetic furnishings, installation of appliances, and necessary partitions, a simple metal box can become a comfortable habitable place for sustainable living. You can actually build your dream home with a shipping container and make it look just as good a home as you've ever desired. In this chapter, we have carefully broken the possible considerations that will aid you in maximizing your container floor space.

Plan 1
Empty Nester

The empty-nester is one of the most popular designs from a custom container home with a 40'/ 320 sq. ft size. It is a comfortable layout space that contains a ground-level bedroom, dining area, a galley kitchen with heavy appliances, a bathtub and many other aesthetics. This is one of the most viable structures that can be built with or without a loft. This home can be built anywhere with a 40' container.

Kitchen:

The kitchen is the highlight of the empty nester with premium counters, tile backsplash, farmhouse deep sink, wooden cabinets. It is a very conducive and comfortable kitchen for practically any cooking activity.

Bathroom:

There are wide options available in selecting a bathroom for your empty nester. In this small space, you have everything you need to have a royal shower. A complete 5' tub shower/combo, LED lights, and wide round bowl toilet. The walls are also painted to match the other walls. You can modify this if you wish.

Living room:

The living room is positioned just right in between the bedroom and the kitchen. It is a joining room. It is designed and structured to harbor a high-top table and enough space for two sofas or a love seat, whichever option you choose.

Bedroom:

The empty-nester allows you to have a main floor bedroom if you wish and another room on the left side. The bedroom space is large enough to fit a queen-size bed and a closet.

Loft area:

The loft area is actually as large as a hallway. It has a ceiling height of 40' for the bathroom, there are large side windows on both sides of the container that allows for plenty of light. It has enough space for a queen-sized mattress.

Exterior:

The exterior of the empty nester can be designed with different designs that can be built with a combination of Faux Stone panels, Siding, and metal sheets.

Plan 2

Happy Twogether

The happy together house model uses a container of 20 inches to create a single bedroom apartment with a sizeable living room, a large kitchen, and a classy 42" walk-in shower bathroom. This building is incredibly awesome for a guest home rental, sportsman cabins, Airbnb, and more.

Kitchen:

The kitchen is built in a galley style that makes it appear open and functional. The kitchen is rightly placed close to the bathroom situated in the second container. You can put in full-size appliances and kitchen equipment without disturbing your comfort.

Bathroom:

The bathroom is situated in the second container, just at the end of the kitchen. It has a 42" walk-in shower toilet with a large storage space for toiletries.

Living room:

If you love the open floor plan concept, the happy-twogether building option is for you. The living room has an open area that is incredibly as wide as one empty container. You would feel roomy once you walk into this space. The open space allowed you home to be positioned in such a place that you have nice early morning views through the glass doors just like in the above picture. It also allows you space to make a burning place.

Bedroom:

This space is big enough to take in a queen-sized bedroom with a good wardrobe corner. There are windows on the three sides that allow in a lot of natural light to give you a homely feel.

Exterior:

You can make replicate the metal sliding design in the image above. It gives it a local and aesthetic look like a solid container home.

Plan 3
Dwell Well

The dwell well design can be achieved with a shipping container of 40' & 20' combined to give a total floor space of 480 sq. ft. The most interesting thing about this structure is the kitchen setup. It is structured in a way that you can cook and serve in the kitchen without many hassles. The unique kitchen design plus foreign aesthetics tend to give you an incredible feel of the entire space and more.

Kitchen:

The kitchen is shaped U and happens to be the only floor plan that allows for a horseshoe kitchen style. This helps to enhance the living space as it allows you to store all of your appliances and cutleries in the right way. It also provides you with more countertops for comfortable kitchen work.

Bathroom:

The bathroom is situated just adjacent to the kitchen and it features a 42" walk-in shower, vanity, toilet and adequate storage. The interior walls are designed to match the walls of other parts of the house.

Living room:

The living/dining space is almost 20' wide. Enough space for a 3-5 family member. You can own this space with the right furniture and make it your dream home. It also allows you sufficient chance to make burning stoves at a corner without choking up the house.

Bedroom:

The bedroom is located on the ground floor with an adequate allowance for a king-size mattress and a top-notch storage closet. You can use a platform like the one in the picture above to position your bed, so you can have storage space underneath.

Exterior:

You have the option of leaving the container exposed or mixing the sidings so that it mixes up well. there would be a single exterior light and a small outlet close to the first door.

Plan 4
Double Duo

This is a one-bedroom and one-bath container home that is built with two shipping containers that are combined together. The bedroom size is as large as a 10'×14' bedroom and it contains a walk-in closet with a full shower structure, leaving you plenty of space for furniture organization and a fully functional kitchen. The double duo design is space-oriented and gives you the opportunity of alternative options in interior structuring and organization. You can also make a second bedroom from the abundance of space you have left if that is your wish.

Kitchen:

This design structure allows you to store a variety of appliances and cooking equipment. Amazingly, it provides kitchen cabinets which also means more countertops for more working hands, giving you the chance to host dinner hangouts in your kitchen. This is a master kitchen indeed.

Bathroom:

Luxury, cozy, and comfortable are sufficient words to describe this amazing bathtub. The bathtub is size 5′ and can contain more than a person at a time. There is also space for a linen cabinet, and a washing machine plus a dryer. What else?

Living room:

This is the heart of the structure. The focus on structure is also applicable here. There is a lot of open spaces, that allow for flexibility in making interior decoration and furniture positioning. You can set up your gaming equipment and fireplace with less stress.

Bedroom:

This bedroom comes with a privacy lock and can accommodate a 32" door. It is a simple 10'×14' bedroom with a standard closet.

Exterior:

The walls are insulated with classic rib gauge metals. The roof is designed aesthetically with a two-tone lap sliding roof material with a solid durability guarantee.

Plan 5

Family Matters 2 Bedroom

This is one of the largest floor plans there is in structuring a shipping container home. This structure gives you wide large spaces with plenty of alternatives with which you can design that limited space. It provides for a large walk-in closet and master bedroom with a 42" shower, toilet and vanity. The second bedroom option provides a 10'×14' floor space with a sizeable walk-in closet. There is a main bathroom that has a 5' shower with a full-size toilet and a double bowl vanity plus a drying and washing machine. Another major highlight is the functional kitchen with enough room with a dining corner and living room space. This container is built with 2 containers of 20 inches and 2 containers of 40 inches to make a total of 960 sq. ft.

Kitchen:

The kitchen is positioned at the center of the back wall in the floor base. There is also provision for cabinet and storage plans in the open one-wall kitchen. The open wall kitchen opens up into the dining and living area to enable you to make the most of your floor space.

Bathrooms:

This structure involves two master bathrooms. The first bathroom which happens to be the main one and positioned in the major living space contains a 5′

shower, space for stacked washer and drying, a very conducive toilet, and a linen cabinet. The second bathroom is positioned in the master bedroom and it has a 42" shower plus a single vanity, and toilet.

Living room:

The living room is positioned directly at the front center of the house right between the two bedrooms. The generous availability of space provides for flexibility for multiple furniture layouts.

Bedroom:

There are two main bedrooms, the master bedroom, and the second bedroom. The master bedroom is 11′×14′ wide and allows plenty of space for a large wardrobe, cabinet and a king-sized bed. The wardrobe is built in such a way to accommodate lots of clothes with a width of 7′×7′. The second bedroom is 10′×14′ with a solid closet. Both rooms come with large windows that allow for plenty of natural light.

Exterior:

There is a lot of different sliding choices for you to combine with or choose from. You could just apply paint to the container to give it an industrial look.

Plan 6
Roommates

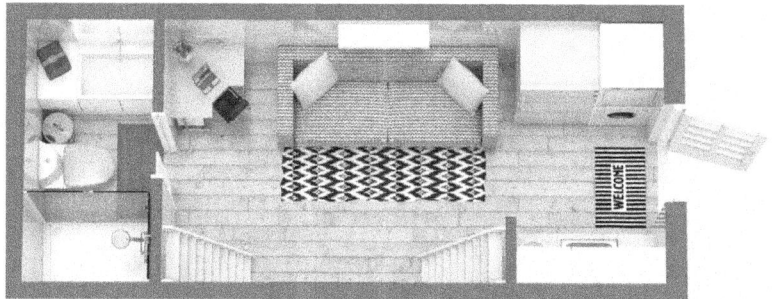

The Roommates layout is a 160 sq. ft space. It is constructed with a container of 20 inches. It provides an option for two separate sleeping lofts large enough for a solid size bed. it also provides adequate space for a kitchenette and bathroom.

This is a very good housing option for campuses, camps, recreation centers, large families, and colleges. In a small space, you can house more people and create structures to help them store their properties well.

Chapter 4

Selecting The Right Container

When you start to consider building your container home, the most important step you can't avoid toying with is getting the right shipping containers. They serve as the walls, floor, roof and general structural support. Do not approach this decision stage with the mind that containers are all the same as long as they serve the purpose. You need to understand that containers vary in quality, price and conditions. You need to be assured that you are paying for the right quality and working conditions you need before structuring your budget.

The size and the quality of the container should be one of the first things you should consider. Will it allow you to use different types of aesthetics? What is the performance level? Is it even with the cost? Is the cost affordable and equivalent to your estimated budget?

Condition is very necessary for consideration when selecting a container. When you select a container with good working conditions, it will be easier to plan your shipping container home and select a workable design. However, a poor container will cost you more and reduce the effect of all your aesthetic designs. Also, you have to draw your design, as it is a guide to helping you select containers that have the specifications you need.

There could be a temptation to buy low-quality containers and to reduce your cost. However, you've got to be conscious of the fact that less quality containers could require more maintenance investment and expenses to put them in place so as to withstand harsh weather conditions.

Importance of Container Condition

You have to determine what quality of containers you need to help you adequately set your chosen building project. Purchasing the right container makes building much easier, as you have fewer requirements and the need for modifications. Your design will help you determine the size of the container that you need, and the quality of the container you need to get.

You also need to determine the condition of the containers without sacrificing quality for cost. You have to put emphasis on the condition of your chosen container type to prevent spending extra on refurbishing your container in the long run. You can determine the condition of containers by inspection or inquiry. There are several types of inspections that you can undergo which will be discussed subsequently.

Right Time to Inspect a Container

As you commence your container home construction, endeavor to take the time to inspect the container yourself. Failure to exercise this duty of care will require that you have to readdress resultant problems and address them at certain points. These can cost incredibly much when repair issues come up. Inspections could be tiring and complex. However, you have to take the pain to inspect these metals before making investments. You can make investments without necessarily making detailed measurements and conditions for more specifications. There are two basic types of inspections. Before we go into discussing them, let us consider the specified details. Your inspection choice is dependent on where you purchase your container. You might not get the chance to inspect your container before delivery. This doesn't mean that inspections are different and the major difference is the time of inspection and the specification of inspection required.

Pre-Purchase Inspection

Inspecting before purchasing your container is best especially if you are close to the location or vendor you will be purchasing from. It is wise you take the pain to go and see it instead of making an order or sending a random individual to get it delivered to you. If the distance is too much for you, you can make a video or photo inspection of the container. Give specifications on how you want the video to be done or the photo to be taken. A live video will be most appropriate.

Post-Purchase Inspection

After the order has been made and the container delivered, you need to check the container to be sure it is in the right shape with the specifications you ordered for. You have to be present to validate your container after it arrives or get someone trusted to do that for you. You don't just receive it and keep it or start working with it without validating its state of arrival. Depending on the mode of operation of the company delivering the containers to you, you'll have to sign off on the delivery. You might not be allowed to inspect the interior on arrival but if there is something wrong with the container, you'll discover it from the exterior. The sooner you discover an issue and report it, the better.

What to Inspect and How?

When setting off to launch your container home, you must take adequate time to do a thorough review of your shipping container yourself. Overlooking this step can expose you to certain dangers in the long run. Although, some contractors could work with lower quality containers and build supplementary designs.

You can adjust your design to allow you to modify damaged areas and use them to make aesthetic decorations or make necessary cuts for windows or doors in that area. The kind of inspection you are required to carry out doesn't involve any special skills, except consciousness and precision in observation. You can create a procedure for carrying out your inspection so you get to miss nothing.

When inspecting visually, scan the container with your heads and eyes in the same direction preferably a direction perpendicular to the path you are working. If you are inspecting a corner scan walking back to front and keep your eyes moving up, down. You can use recording tools like a long selfie stick that will allow you to take videos of locations and parts, your eyes cannot assess. Another tool you'll need is a flashlight and a ladder to give you full visual experience, and a hammer to check for rust.

- Structural frame: the strength of a container is based on the 12 steel beams situated at the six edges. These beams come in different sizes dependent on the rail structure. Damage on the beam is almost unfixable. They tend to contain deep cross-sections. Hence to get a view of their true state, you'd have to assess it from inside and outside. Your concern should be on deeper rust because it is a sign of corrosion, which reduces the beam's strength. Surface rust poses little or zero risks.

- Underside: this part of the container is invisible to the eye upfront but it is made up of small beams that stretch through the container length. This is where you screw your plywood into. Because this part is permanently hidden from the sun which should dry it when it gathers moisture, it is almost impossible to prevent it from rusting. However, you could take advantage of the time in between when the container is being moved from the delivery vehicle to the mapped-out layout portion, and take snapshots. If you miss this opportunity, you might have to hire an equipment to lift the container up. Nonetheless, damage in this area can easily be repaired without hampering your aesthetics.

- Walls: a container has four rectangular walls that are very much visible to the eye for inspection. The container is enveloped in corrugated steel that helps to sustain its structural stamina. Surface rust can be a challenge if it is too severe, it will be hard to cover up. Also, if there is a see-through hole on any side of the walls, it could be a sign that the container is really weak and wider holes are bound to come out at a time. However, you can take advantage of the damaged work areas to make door and window cuts. Also, note that dents that are robust enough to be visible can interrupt your container designs. Container walls are usually deep, when a dent goes deep enough to be visible on the side, there is a situation.

- Roof: you can inspect the top of the container with your selfie stick or use a ladder to inspect. You should be on the lookout for fair conditions like signs of stagnant water, old patches, and dents. You can also use the hammer test here but be careful to not put your body weight on an area that has been weakened by rust. You can only tell if the roof is waterproof when you check the interior.

- End doors: this is the only access point to your container. Note that part of a structure that moves might get weak and become obsolete when affected by dirt and corrosion. Check the hinges, all four lock bars, and the lock, observe how they spin. Also, check the perimeter of the doors for missing parts that need to be replaced.

- Interior: this is a continuation of the exterior inspection to validate all that you saw on the outside and ensure that the interior is waterproof. Check the walls and roofs with your flashlight to enhance your view. To find out if there are openings in the walls, close the odors and feed your eyes on how to fix them. Use spray pipes to confirm the waterproof feature. Hence, you can patch your roof with the right materials once you identify faults.

- Floor: this is another section you need to pay full attention to. The most permeable floor material commonly used is plywood. This means that it easily absorbs toxic chemicals.

Documentation

When securing your shipping container, certain documentation is important or necessary to acquire. One of them is discussed below;

- CSC Plate: in some locations, it is also regarded as Combined Data Plate and it is the most detailed part of the container. This data is on a single metal plate that is permanently glued to the container. Under this CSC plate, there are specific information that is worthy of note.

    1. Container identification Number: also termed BIC Code, this number is built together with an equipment identifier, check digit, serial number, and owner prefix. It is an identification number that points out the owner and the vehicle. The check digit helps you to verify the correctness of the Container Identification Number.

2. Type code: this code is made up of 4 distinct digits. In some cases, it is a mix-up of letters and codes. For instance, 42G1 means average height, general-purpose and 40-foot container.

3. Classification Society Approval: certain societies approved the container before it got to you, this number includes a reference to this approval organization.

4. ACEP/PES: the CSC plate will definitely have enough space for an ACEP number and follow-up PES examinations. This ACEP number is usually in correspondence with the classification society approval code.

Conditions and Container Grades

The highest standard that validates containers is the CSC certification. Besides this, there is no other validation. Hence, it could be difficult to grade a container adequately. There are different certification and validation grades. Some intra category grades have been created for containers by certain companies, however, they cannot be trusted because these categorizations were placed on one side by one person's perception.

When assessing a container that is placed on sale and has been categorized by an expert, you are expected to get an understanding of the seller's position in determining the condition and grade of the container. While you examine different seller's classifications and grading, you need to understand why it was made so in the first place. You can sign off a deal that will allow you to regain your money if the container doesn't meet your specifications. Also, note that these categorizations are based on aesthetics and cosmetics in place of structural implications. When assessing lower quality containers, you need to determine if the wears and slight damages affect the condition of the container's structure. Not all sellers use grades, so we'll divide the container types into two. They will be discussed further below;

New (and New-ish) Containers

These are brand new containers that are either one-trip, refurbished and clean new. Refurbished is a tricky term to use here as no standard covers for it. In some situations, it is also categorized as used. You can categorize it yourself after understanding to a balanced level the steps involved in the refurbishment.

One-Trip Containers

This container is sometimes likened to the category of new containers. However, this container is commonly used to move a single cargo load from the manufacturing company in a country to another country. After fulfilling this service, these containers are packed up for sale. You can bet that it is as good as new. There are only complications when there are situations of mishandling. In many locations, you are certain to get one-trip containers for small money.

Refurbished Containers

Refurbishment is a word that describes bringing the old to new or dead to life. It must have gone through a process of repair, restoration, and review. However, refurbishment is also limited to aesthetics restructuring. Over the years, container owners have stopped refurbishing due to the excessive cost required. Many of them just decide to replace, as it is a much cheaper option. Refurbishments are now conducted by local sellers or resellers, not users. Sometimes, refurbishments could make a container not be in correspondence with the CSC certification because it might still have some poorly patched areas and replacement parts. The difference between a new and refurbished container is quite easy to tell. Their performance which is the main center of focus cannot be decided except upon verification. Refurbishments might include removal of rusts, dents, scratches, repainting and priming. It might also require the replacement of doors and revamping an entire wall. However, the fact remains that it is much affordable to get a good container than trying to refurbish an old one and make it look new.

Used Containers

These are containers that have exhausted a large part of their useful life. There are usually categorized by barely used and completely used up. Containers do not basically have expiry dates but if used for a very long time, they can start to wear and tear, and eventually become risky for use at the time of depreciation. It makes no sense to invest at this point as the wear and time would never end until the container is condemned. Most containers in this category are those that have been repaired or refurbished at a point. However, the repair can only hold it together for a long while before it all rusts and become useless.

Cargo Worthy (CW) Containers

These containers are categorized and certified by CSC certificates. This categorization implies that the container has a performance standard of a high percentage when compared to the details in the original specification. They might not be appealing to the eyes but they are as strong or almost as standard as new containers. They are confirmed to be in better shape than most used containers. However, modifying their exterior by cutting would make the certificate invalid.

As-Is Containers

These are less standard containers when compared to cargo-worthy containers. The As-Is have many cosmetics and aesthetics defects that it is fairly encouraging to purchase. When purchasing this container, you would need to be on-site to see the nature and level of defects and determine if it is good enough for your project. This container is known for different types of wear and tear, and it is never sold on warranty, so the risk of danger or accident upon purchase is fully borne by you. However, it could still prove to be a really good bargain.

Why Choose New (and New-ish) Containers?

- Uniformity: when you purchase a couple of these containers for your building project, it is easy to get them set up together without having to bend or make many cuts for alignment and uniformity sake. You would save a lot of money you would have spent on modification, painting, removal and repairs that would most certainly come with purchasing a used container.

- Appearance: they are appealing to the eyes, and attractive to behold. You can keep them in your yard without raising awkward stares from nosy neighbors.

- Life span: you have a sure guarantee for long useful life before modification is required.

- Peace of mind: although, used containers can be less disturbing and more intensive after modification, the assurance that your container is in good shape gives you rest and peace of mind that you can use it to set up any project that you intend. You can set up any house structure of your choice without fear of unforeseen dangers.

Why Choose Used Containers?

- Affordability: this is the major reason 90% of the persons who bought used containers do so. Used containers pose as a cheaper alternative to acquiring a shipping container for whatever purpose.

- Availability: you can find a used container very close to your geographical location without much stress because most companies happen to use and dump shipping containers when they are done. Getting a new or high-quality container might require you to travel for long hours to the port to get one for yourself. You can find your container early and start setting up your building structure early.

- Eco-friendliness: reuse is always beneficial to the environment and helps to keep the environment safe because you are not gathering materials to rebuild. You are building with already existent materials; this is called adaptive reuse or recycling. In some developed states, you might get a certification for green building or tax evasion incentive to appreciate your goodwill.

Cost of Shipping Containers

Prices of shipping containers differ based on condition (new, new-ish, or used), type (height, length), age, and location. Nonetheless, the prices are always closely related. We have computed an average price level or bracket for getting a shipping container in any location or quality of your choice. It is not a sure price, remember it is only an estimate. You might get your container for a cheaper or more affordable price.

- Used Standard 20 foot container: US$2,100
- Newish Standard 20foot container: US$3,000
- Used Standard 40foot container: US$2,850
- Newish Standard 40foot Container: US$5,600
- Used High Cube 20foot Container: US$2,200
- Newish High Cube 20foot Container: US$3,200
- Used High Cube 40foot Container: US$2,950
- Newish High Cube 40foot Container: US$5,800

Shipping Container Condition to Buy?

Now that you have come to understand the different container conditions and their implications, as well as their pros and cons, you should be able to decide on the container that is best for you and the structure of your project. Here are a few questions to help you select your container condition and make a purchase decision.

1. Will you need to move your container?

If your answer is yes, you should be on the lookout for CW containers.

2. Do you intend to build in large windows and doors?

If yes, carefully engage in inspection before purchase to avoid any weakness on the main support beam.

3. Will you be opening a whole part of the container walls to allow for larger open space?

If yes, ensure upon your inspection that the main support beams are in a good shape.

4. Will you use a separate corrugated sheet for roofing?

If yes, you should be less bothered about damages discovered on the roof of the container.

5. Are you particular about cosmetics and aesthetics?

If yes, then you should consider a new container or budget for refurbishing a used container to your taste.

6. Do you intend on replacing the floor or modifying the container floor to more standard?

If yes, the damages on the plywood floors should bother you less

Buying Your Containers

When you are deciding on the quality of shipping containers, it could be difficult making your selection when you are ready. Prices could be scary and you don't know how to trust the result of your inspection. Also, different sellers deal in shipping containers ranging from dealers, resellers, distributors, and middlemen, and all of these persons have their own processes. However, once you have decided finally on the condition and quality of the container you want to get, the work is made easier. The next decision stage is deciding where you want to buy your container.

Most business purchases are now done online. The internet is now a full-fledged marketplace. Hence, you can focus your search online. Finding a container offline is not impossible but it could be difficult.

Online - In The US:

If you live in the United States, check out BoxHub. This is a website that allows you to find containers nationwide, conduct your inspections, evaluate pricing levels, and make your complete purchase. In certain circumstances when you happen to be less satisfied with the order upon delivery, they provide a refund policy. They have a team that works in direct relations with specific shipping companies across the nation and stand as middlemen to help them sell off the containers to individuals or retailing companies. They tend to deliver quality at a lower cost when compared with other companies. They also coordinate delivery constructively at a very affordable rate.it is proven to be an easier way to purchase your container online in the US than using Amazona and many sophisticated seller options. If you are unable to connect with BoxHub, you can check out other companies in the outer space that are also keen on quality and affordability. You could also use your city code to search on google. Make a search like; shipping container + London. You can use the name of a particular city in your state for a more narrowed search. If you are settling for striking the purchase deal with an individual or firm that is not registered as a container dealer, you might have to travel over there for physical inspection to validate its quality and arrange for delivery logistics afterward.

Online - Outside The US:

No matter your location, every country has access to shipping containers. There is surely a way to track down a container that you need, either on a seaport or container terminal. You can find seaports using the Sea rate website. You will find several seaports alongside information about their operations. You can inquire from there if they sell containers and their price ranges. If you leave too far from the coast, a land port option is best considered for you. You can check out options close to you using Craiglist or Gumtree. Most commonwealth companies have major ad sites for trading containers. Ensure to conduct a broad search before settling for any decision. Take the time to scroll through all available results and validate the results with the condition, quality, and cost requirements you have. One-trip containers can mostly be secured in Asia, you can get in touch with container dealers from that region through Alibaba. Although, it is more costly and stressful, as you have to do a lot of paperwork and inspections but you are sure of getting a high-quality container.

Finding Containers Offline:

There are a lot of container dealers in space that you might not actually find until you start searching. Some businesses and individuals just have containers sitting around their vicinity that they don't know what to do with it. If you notice any container lying around, you can look for the owner and strike a bargain for purchase. Some of them might be pretty glad at the prospects of clearing their yard for money. This is an incredibly good catch you wouldn't want to miss, so keep your eyes open.

You can take advantage of personal referrals from people you know in the shipping or logistics industry. If you contact any dealer within your location who failed to help you strike a deal, ensure to ask for a connection to another until you find the container you want.

Choosing a Container Dealer

Choosing a container dealer is almost as important as choosing a container because when you set out to buy a container, you are establishing a business relationship. Also, there are a lot of container dealers out there, you want to be guaranteed that you are dealing with the right one.

Integrity and Reputation:

In selling transactions, the term knowledge asymmetry is used to describe the fact that most sellers are more knowledgeable than the buyers as regards the subject of the transaction. Hence, you have to find a trustworthy seller that won't look for ways to play on your ignorance and rip you off your money for a low-quality product. You can easily evaluate the trustworthiness of a seller by checking out their membership in organizations in the industry like Container Dealer's Association, Intermodal Association of North America, National Portable Storage Association, and many others. This doesn't totally validate a seller but it gives validation to a level of trust and faith.

You can also consider finding out other buyers' opinions through buyer's reviews online or inquires from people in your area who have made certain purchases from a container dealer. Finally, you can also establish trust by verifying your purchase. At the point of price agreement, take note of the CSC plate information and after the container is delivered do a check to confirm if it is the one you selected.

Warranties and Returns:

Demanding a warranty and return allowance upon dissatisfaction is a good bet you can bid for. Note that it is only a trustworthy seller that would consider giving you a warranty offer. Some warranty offers come with extended fees on rare occasions. If you don't want to make the payment, you can forgo the purchase altogether as it could be a red flag sign. although, warranties could be invalid when you are ordering a shipping container to build a home. Ensure to read up the warranty offer before making the payment for the purchase, and ensure to understand the terms and conditions applied to avoid unpleasant stories.

Volume Discounts:

Discounts are only applicable when you are purchasing more than one container. It is wise to buy all the containers you need from a certain vendor to enable you to bid for a discount and makes your record-keeping easier. In some cases, the seller openly discloses them and in other cases, you might have to demand for it with a negotiation before making payment. Discounts are only applicable to volume pricing which is an important concept in business marketing. Here are two things you need to be educated about before striking off a discount negotiation.

1. Average Customer Value (ACV): what is the revenue or turnover rate a single customer generates for the company.

2. Customer Acquisition Cost (CAC): what are the required expenses a company incurs in getting a single paying customer.

You might not have the numbers; a good estimation is enough. If you are buying many containers, you are saving the company's ACV in getting a new customer. Hence, it is only reasonable that the company reduces your purchasing expenses by giving you a discount. If you are good at negotiation, you might strike a good bargain and save yourself some money.

Value-Added Services:

There are regular sellers and value-added sellers. Regular sellers just sell off their commodities to you. Value-added sellers help you to put the commodity to use after selling it off to you. They might charge you for rendering these services because they are necessary but it is worth the extra penny. Some of the extra services that are common in container sales are delivery and offloading. Others are modification and set up which includes, painting, installation, insulation, and welding. You have the option of letting your container dealer do it for you or hiring a contractor. Before you settle for any of the decisions, make inquiries and find out the quality of service rendered by your container dealer, and compare it with your contractor's work with their prices.

Delivery and Offloading:

When selecting a container dealer, look out for those that can help you coordinate the logistics or you might have to engage in finding out companies that can assist in logistics. Large container dealers possess necessary equipment for delivery and offloading that smaller companies or dealers might not have. Once the delivery is set, be cleared on the processes, the responsibility of offloading and security of container during transit.

Another factor to consider is the time of delivery. Anyone that is trustworthy can deliver a product but the question is When? How long will it take to get ten containers delivered to your geographical location? Although, most sellers cannot give you an accurate forecast because business is dynamic and sometimes the future is not really measurable and could come unexpectedly. They might not get orders early to deliver alongside your order. Just get familiar with their terms of operation.

Chapter 5

Preparation of Site and Foundation

Preparation of Site

Now that you have understood how to select a container for building, you need to also prepare the building site for construction even before the container is delivered to your location. The site preparation at this stage is bordered around the need to prepare your chosen location and make it ready for building. You are also to prepare the site with the building design in mind. It might be quite tasking to align your site to your design but just like every other stage, this stage is definitely surmountable.

Choosing Your Location

After considering the thought of building a container home, the next thing you need to do is deciding the particular site where your container home will be located. This is a decision you have to settle in your mind before starting to take basic actions.

Sun and Shade:

Depending on the weather situation in your location, the sun could be an exciting element or a punishment. Practically, sun and shade are best if you are keen on natural light and early morning warmth from sunrise. Nonetheless, this doesn't exempt the harshness and heat that could come about in the afternoon when the weather is pretty unfriendly.

Note how the sun rises and falls, its tenacity and harshness at each time of the day and in different areas of peculiar locations. Also, shades from trees or bushes could help reduce the heat and harshness of the sunrays from penetrating your building, but it could also affect the elevation of the horizon. During winter, these shades could disappear and fall away. The sun has different temperatures or reactions at different times of the year, some of them favorable, some of them unfavorable. However, you can discover varying sun behavior at different horizons, in different seasons using Sun Calc. This can also help you in structuring your design in a way to reduce the effect of the sun on your building like creating overhangs for your doors and windows.

Topography and Drainage:

Topography refers to the positioning or structure of the land, drainage is how water moves through the land. A poor topography will give your container home imbalance and put it in danger of the wind and strong winter seasons. You might need to purchase or construct a foundation system under your container to keep it stable. Poor drainage areas could also expose your container to rust and create deep dents in your container. Even when it is not affecting the container, it could create a breeding space for mosquitos, snakes, and bugs. You would not want to fall prey to these creatures, so inspect your topographical and drainage system well.

Views:

Does your location allow you to have top views into your compound, the parking yard, the city, or the garden? Your windows, doors, and corridors will most certainly be facing a location. What location will that be? Is it inspiring or captivating enough as you desire it to be? This is considering your view from inside to outside but you also need to consider your outside to inside view. What do outsiders see when they pass, can they get a view of your bedroom, bathroom or living room? This could be quite an issue. Another view you should consider is the view of your home from the street. What orientation does your home give on the map? Will it be parallel or perpendicular? This will not just help you to structure and determine your device location, you will also be able to determine the right design for your container home.

Access:

How do you intend to access your house? Except you want to go off-grid, your access should be through an automobile. The basic road you can build can be straight and short but what if you don't have that much space? You can first take the pain to calculate how long it will take you to access your property from the main street and ensure there is no disastrous steep or obstacle to be avoided. You might need to remove the obstacle totally if it is a tree.

When thinking of access, you should also estimate access space or route for the construction machinery and vehicles not just your personal car. Will they be able to beat the muds, and bends to enter into your land space. You might need to alter your access route for the sake of construction then readapt afterward. What matters is that you have access to your building when you wish to.

Site Work

This section would address all the physical work that you need to do to get your building site ready. It only makes sense to break these site work into parts so you don't injure yourself or cause any damage.

Marking and Staking:

The basic step here is using marking tools to highlight the corners where your container home will be built and constructed. It also involves determining the location of utilities and roads, amongst other things.

You would need the assistance of a utility company before you commence anything. They will help you with a guide on the required utilities that are affiliated and required by your property. You can mark these points using wood stakes or marking paints or connecting them with strings.

Clearing and Grubbing:

Next, you need to clear out the marked space. Clearing out here might involve the destruction of vegetation, cutting down of trees and removal of debris. This is something you can do yourself, or pay a contractor to do it for you if you are keen on a faster and neater job. If your location is sited in a vegetation or a bushy area, you might require heavy equipment to make quality clear-outs. You don't have to throw away everything from your clear-out, you can select through them and reuse them, an example is reusing a small flower for gardening or making a corn post with it. The debris alongside other junks should be disposed of at the dumpsite.

Grading, Cut, and Fill:

Now that everything is probably cleared out of your way, you have a blank open site. You can see the fullness and the end of your entire land space. Depending on your chosen design, you can start to structure your foundation. If you intend on using a slab, this is the time to get it and position it because your container would be dropped directly on it. However, you need to level your ground and make sure every corner is even. Clear outs could make your ground uneven and broken up, it could eventually lead to erosion is not handled properly. Now, you have to also set up your drainage flow with beams until the house is completely built. You might also need to do some work on the access road so the contractors can easily access your site. Fill the bumps and steepen the grades. You might have to build a bridge where the road is too bad or to create a passage over a strong water flow.

Road Building:

You can take this advantage and begin to construct a more functional road. This building might require you to purchase gravel, asphalt, road base and concrete to make it durable and strong. You might need the help of a contractor and heavy equipment to do this. However, you will most certainly thank yourself at the end.

Erosion Control:

After clearing out space for building, you would have a lot of space that could be befitting for erosion attract just as we have discussed above. During rain falls, the topper part of the soil is constantly washed away and the ground is made uneven. You can plant vegetation upon locations that you know are viable by erosion. Also, you can make use of erosion control devices like blankets or silt fences. You can get further help from your environmental quality office.

Fencing and Security:

At this point, your building project has started. You will most certainly be working with heavy tools that you cannot keep moving back and forth, you might have to leave some of your equipment on site. Your container can act as a good security place. If you are yet to have your container on the property, you can consider building a fence or setting up a security camera. Basically, put up any legal structure that helps you to secure the safety of your tools and equipment.

Foundation

Is Foundation Necessary for Containers?

This topic of debate is very necessary after you must have established your container design. However, you need to realize that the ground is not always steady, it is viable by environmental factors that can make it sleep, slide, sink or rise hence destabilizing the balance of your home. Setting up a foundation helps you to withstand all of these reactions and keeps the container stable, firm and solid. It will also ensure the weight of your container is well distributed. Since it prevents your container from having direct contact with the soil, your container is shielded from corrosion which could arise from moisture.

Foundation Types for Containers

There are four main foundation types used in building container homes, they are all discussed below;

Pier Foundation:

This inexpensive foundation option is the most popularly used because it is easy and quick to construct. This foundation consists of concrete blocks, measured to be about 50cm ×50cm×50cm. These piers are laid at every corner of the container. You can place an additional pier midway for a container as large as 40-foot. You don't need to do any evacuation work, just arrange and set up. No need for digging up the earth or for heavy equipment. With your hands, you can set up your foundation in no time.

Pile Foundation:

This foundation type is commonly used when the soil is tested to be weak and unable to hold a concrete base in place. It is the most expensive option. Here, the piles which happen to be round solid steel tubes are inserted into the ground with hammers until the piles are stuck at a more stable ground level. Then it is secured firmly on that spot with a large block of concrete. You do this at every corner until you have secured all your piles underground. It cannot be done by a DIY builder; you need to use some complex tool like a plier driver.

Slab Foundation:

This is another choice for a weak soft ground. Here, the strategy used is equal weight distribution. If not well articulated and planned, it could prove to be more difficult to build than a pier foundation. You would need to do a lot of digging which is a really unpleasant task. The slab is a large concrete, sometimes larger than the footprint of the container upon which the container is placed. For a 40-foot container, your slab would be 42 foot long. It creates an overhanging perimeter for your home which could add to your container home aesthetics. It is much more stable and sustainable than the other options. However, it reduces or limits your reachability to utility lines. When there is a leak in the container through one of the pipes it is very stressful to fix together.

Strip Foundation:

This foundation is also known as a trench foundation. It is usually the combination of a pier and slab foundation. It is basically a construct of a strip of concrete which is usually 4 feet deep and 1-2 feet wide.

This strip can be placed around the perimeters of the containers, or directly at the bottom. It is a cheaper and weaker option when compared to the slab foundation. Studies have it that it has low or zero resistance to natural disasters like earthquakes. The strip foundation is best used when building small or medium container sizes.

Strength of Foundation Concrete to Use

If you are using a pier or slab foundation which happens to be both concrete, you'd need to measure the strength of the concrete that you would use. Basically, you cannot determine this yourself. You'd need the help of a geotechnical engineer to examine the land and make his report before you can decide on the concrete strength.

Concrete strength is referred to as C. the multi-purpose concrete which most persons use is C15 concrete. It is usually compacted by 2 parts sand, 1-part cement, and 5 parts gravel. The higher the number of cement, the stronger the concrete. C30 is a stronger concrete that includes 1-part cement, 2 parts sand, and 3 parts gravel.

You can mix your concrete mechanically or with a concrete mixer. If it is more than 1 cubic meter, you can order the concrete to be mixed somewhere and delivered to your site. To calculate the number of cubic meters you need for a 10-foot-wide container, that is 22-foot long and 2-foot deep slab, multiply the numbers together; 22×10×2. This will give you 440. That is the number of cubic feet you need to order.

Ensure the cement is well mixed with water and every other necessary element. This will help it to maintain durability and stability. Note that concrete cures in 5-7 days. Do not do any work around the container while you allow the concrete to cure.

How to Attach Containers to Foundations

Steel plate is a common way of attaching foundation to a container. It involves pressing a steel plate into wet concrete. You have the option of using mechanical anchors or totally epoxying the anchor. A flat concrete plate fitting for the container size should be placed at the four sides of the container. After the concrete is solid enough. The containers should be established and solidified on the steel plate then everything should be welded together.

Instead of going through all of this stress, you can place your container directly on the foundation and allow it to find balance by its massive weight. however, you would stand in the danger of natural disasters and chaos.

Chapter 6

Container Insulation

What is Insulation?

Insulation is the installation and fixing of certain materials that help to make your room or building more comfortable by protecting you from extreme outdoor temperatures. This is what makes your home comfortable in the summer when you can't bear to spend one more minute outside. You'll want to ensure that the air in your space is conditioned, and comfortable to take in irrespective of the season. Not every structure or material has the ability to give your room this warm and welcoming atmosphere. Thin materials or structures cannot prevent harsh weather conditions like rain, snow, or sun from making your home inhabitable. Insulation is practically the material that is being installed in your home to trap air from harsh weather conditions from permeating through the walls of your home. Of all elements, gases are proven to inefficiently conduct thermal energy, this makes them great insulators. Thermal insulation basically refers to controlling heat flow conductively. When measuring the resistance to heat flow, you can use the R-value.

Reason to Insulate Your Container?

Insulation helps you to preserve your inner airspace from harsh weather conditions. It reduces the amount of energy that would be required for you to regulate and control your container's temperature. Insulation is very important in building but much more important in building a shipping container home. Containers are more viable to harsh temperature conditions because of the steel. They could help to preserve the inner parts from cold weather conditions but they perform worse in warm-weather conditions and lead to high heat radiation. Basically, insulation is necessary to reduce the harshness of climate on the container interior.

The Effect of Climate on Your Choice of Insulation

Locations with harsh weather conditions require serious insulation. In summer, when the sun is all out and blazingly hot, you can make use of fans, air conditions, or warm clothing to withstand the heat. However, it could be quite unbearable in winter, cold is harsher than heat and even a warm fireplace can provide little help at such moments. You might have to compare the cost of continuous heating or cooling with the cost of insulating. You would realize that, unlike the cooling and heating option which involves continuous expenses, the insulation fee is a one-time cost.

The fact remains that using a heating or cooling option could make you burn more money. Insulation gives you comfort at a much affordable one-time cost price. Note that, failure to insulate your container could also expose it to water condensation. Which may in turn lead to mold or corrosion.

How to Place Your Container Insulation

Insulating a container might require fixing up several layers of materials to provide a level of fire resistance and vapor barrier. You will have to determine your container skin location in the wall system. The best option is to place insulation inside the container as it is most effective. You can add these insulation materials with studs just in between using cavities.

You could also use an exterior insulation option. The materials that you would use here would have to be water-resistant with solid sheathing. The major advantage of exterior insulation is more space for interior décor and storage units.

Choosing Your Insulation

When choosing a shipping container insulation option, you have to be mindful of the pros and cons as these insulation options can modify the condition of your shipping containers. Although, these insulation options could vary depending on your location and region. Here are a few factors you should put into consideration when deciding on an insulation option.

- Overall performance: characteristics underperformance is generally affected by entrapped gas, and closed-cell structure.

- R-value: the ability or quality of the material to prevent the transmission or passage of heat energy.

- Air leakage: to what extent does the insulation option reduce the passage of air through the material.

- Vapor permeability: how well does the insulation option prevent vapor from passing through it.

- Cost: the cost is fixed based on its ease of installation, and the required tools.

- Eco-friendliness: the materials tend to vary the ecological impacts of their installation.

Types of Insulation for Containers

There are majorly five insulation types for your container. They are grouped by the physical form they take which is directly synchronized to their method of application. Some insulation materials can fit into two or more categories of insulation. However, you must understand the differences between materials and how they relate to your personal circumstances.

Non-Traditional: the materials under this category are unconventional, affordable and eco-friendly. They are less suitable for R-value owners as they take much room space. They are most suitable for extreme climate conditions. Examples of such types are listed below;

- Strawbale: the straws, in this case, can be likened to the bale used in feeding a horse, and they can be stacked together like blocks. It is best used on the exterior of the container.

- Hempcrete: this material is likened to concrete but it is made with hemp which poses lesser strength than concrete.

Blanket: this insulation option comes in rolls of different sizes and lengths. You would have to cut it after measurement before making an installation for insulation. Much like the regular sleeping blanket, this blanket is soft, fluffy and compressible. It is most effective in keeping warm on cold days. It is usually installed with studs and cavities to ensure its structural stamina. This is a very cheap option and it is quite easy to use. Note that you might need to install a vapor retarder alongside as the blanket is permeable by water vapor. Examples are;

- Fiberglass insulation: this is made from heated sand or reprocessed glass that is cut into tinny small fibers. In developed countries, this is common and cheap.

- Slag wool: unlike fiberglass, this blanket is made from slag which happens to be a metal byproduct.

- Sheep wool: this insulation is made from the shearing of wool from sheep.

- Cotton insulation: this is a blanket that is made from cotton-like clothes material.

Loose-Fill: this is uniquely different and involves the application of small bits of insulating devices termed media into a wall cavity. Generally, the insulators need a full wall cavity containment before application.

- Cellulose insulation: this is made from shredded recycled products that are blown into the machine.

- Loose-fill fiberglass insulation: it is quite similar to fiberglass but it is thicker and cannot be easily blown into the machine.

- Perlite insulation: these are materials like mineral that has been modified to expand to the shape and size of popcorn. Hence, they can be used as natural foam pellets to be added to wall cavities.

Expanded Foam: this is almost similar to blanket insulation as it is soft and compressible also. However, it involves the manufacturing of foam on large boards and measured wall heights. You can simply make holes for necessities like windows and doors on-site by cutting. This insulation strategy can be done by anyone by attaching these boards with studs or simply gluing them to the container. It is usually molded to match the shapes of the container wall. They are known to have the highest R-value for every inch.

- Open Cell PU Foam: these foams are usually filled with air and do not always go dense like that. It also comes with a sponge-like texture and an unequal level of R-value.

- Closed Cell PU Foam: this is a tiny agent that fills microscopic cells and has a gas that's different from air and possesses higher heat conduction requirements or properties.

- Extruded Polystyrene Foam: just like the little white foams that form on the surface of your hot coffee, this foam contains tiny plastic beads that easily fuse together.

- Expanded Polystyrene Foam: here, molten materials are pressed with so much pressure to make a closed-cell foam sheet.

- Polyiso: this is quite similar to the open-cell foam but it is more rigid.

Spray: this can be produced from spraying materials like liquid mixture which eventually hardens and becomes solid. It is usually continuous and could be made to expand into different nooks, cracks, and crannies. It becomes thick enough to prevent the transfer of heat and restrict air movement. It tends to expand more and more upon application before it eventually hardens.

- Open-cell spray polyurethane foam: it has a low R-value and allows for air movements just in the middle of cells.

- Closed-cell spray polyurethane foam: this is the most common type of container insulation people in average climate condition areas use. It contains a very high R-value and provides strong vapor retardation. You have to be mindful of protecting the gas after spraying because they could escape and lead to a reduction in the R-value of the spray.

There is also the non-expanding spray insulation option to consider. Unlike the spray foams listed above, it doesn't move around but you can still move it round to fill the cavity totally.

- Damp spray cellulose insulation: this is made from paper products that have been recycled and shredded. It contains a unique rig that allows for the application of water and adhesives at the spraying point. This helps the cellulose to stay bind together on the open-sided wall cavities.

- Cementitious Foam Insulation: this involves an extremely light mixture of air, water and minerals that after being mixed looks like cured concrete. You have to apply it and allow it to cure before making any modification. You need not worry about your safety, cementitious foam is non-toxic, eco-friendly and non-flammable with good R-value quality.

Chapter 7

Container Movement and Delivery

Getting your container delivered and installed right on your site could be one of the most challenging and frustrating tasks in building a container home. Transporting it yourself might be a whole lot of stress, the best bet is to contract a logistics company or your container dealer to handle the nitty-gritty with the delivery This delivery process requires several types of clearance and a loop some amount of money tagged delivery charges. In delivery, distance and quantity is the key. Short distances are always more affordable than long distances.

Moving a Shipping Container Across Your Property

The distance referred to here is a few hundred feet. Most companies find it strenuous to bring out instruments and equipment just to move a container within a short distance and spend just a short while carrying out the task. However, it is still not something you can do yourself except you have all the required equipment. A single 20' pounds container is said to weigh about 5000 pounds. You cannot push this with your hands, at all. You can only make a drag through the road or a grassy area till you get to your site but this could lead to wears on your container or unpleasant marks on the road. It would also be very stressful for the tower towing the container to keep up. A better DIY option is to jack it and position it on something that would enable it to roll. Another considerable option is placing special brackets on the corners to allow you to mount car wheels on the container. If you have access to a bulldozer, you can put two wheels at one end of it. All these DIYs are only practicable if you have a tractor any large towing equipment. The cost of moving your container across your property is estimated at $1,000 and the timing is just a few hours.

Moving a Shipping Container Across Your City

Moving your container across the city is quite a tedious job and requires that you hire a trailer or a chassis used in holding shipping containers. This can only be hired from professionals, so you know how to sketch your search. In a decent city, you might find a company that trades shipping containers, you can strike a deal/bargain with them. if you intend on moving a container already sited on your property to another location, you might have to jump the big rope of finding a trailer because you have to first load your container into a trailer or chassis before it can be moved. There should be a contain yard around, they have this equipment. If you can't find one, your best bet would be hiring a crane. The cost is estimated at around $1-$4 per mile. The time is estimated for driving time using google maps to track the exact timing plus the time spent loading and unloading.

Moving a Shipping Container Across Your State or Country

This movement usually involves thousands and hundreds of miles but in some sense, it is not always different from the normal movement across the city. It basically requires the same process, instrument and tactics. The major difference is the company that would be helping you with the delivery. The normal local companies who would have assisted you through intercountry or state movement, are not licensed to move internationally or cross-country. What this implies for the drivers is that they will be driving long miles to deliver your container and have to make the long return back empty, with no commissioned delivery.

You would want to save yourself a whole lot of stress and hire a professional trucking or delivery company.

they have equipment that can transport your equipment for several miles without breaking down or wearing out. They also have the connections to get them a return commission so they don't get to return empty-handed. You can find these companies on the following platforms;

- uShip: this online platform allows you to search for haulers through listings.
- Local Hauler: this platform is affiliated with a google search. It streams your search to haulers in your location.
- Freight agent: freight agents usually have a list of load boards and haulers in different locations. You can look at this list and select the companies in your location. You can also make a google search using your city name plus freight brokerage.

Make sure that you are well informed on the terms of delivery, insurance, and contract of carriage. This cost is usually $1-$4 per mile. The time is also measured by google maps and the required loading and unloading.

Moving a Shipping Container Across The World

The move of this scale might involve ocean trips and rail trips. This situation might require that you get involved in various transport services. It always comes with logistical complexity because you will have to deal with travel agents of different borders and customs officers of different states. The best platform to get a hauler for this kind of contract is a Freight Brokerage. The overall cost for transacting this business is dependent on the weight of freight rates. The time taken to transport a container across the world might be months or long weeks.

Preparing a Container For Movement

When you want to get a container delivered or relocated, there are a few preparations you need to make.

1. Align the weight: there is a maximum gross weight for moving equipment, before moving your container, check to know the gross weight for moving container in your area. You might need to check the weight of the equipment used in loading, and the capacity of the wheels that will be attached to the truck used in puling it. it

might be impossible to get the accurate weight of the containers. You might have to make an estimate. Most manufacturers indicate the weight of their container on the package. If your container's weight is larger than the weight of your equipment.
2. Secure items: when you intend to move your container, you need to know that things will most certainly be bumping around. Hence, you need to secure every item that you will be placed on the container to prevent it from being damaged. In securing these items, you might need to tie them in place or weld them to the wall of the container.
3. Inventory contents: make sure to take inventory of the condition of your container and the contents before setting it on the road. This will give you a good record of everything that is lost or damaged in the face or eventuality of an accident. First of all, take note of the actual condition of your container, and its contents. You might need to take plenty of pictures to help you to take accurate stock of this. Also, you can record the CSC or any other number on the container to ensure you receive the container you ordered.

Loading and Offloading Your Shipping Containers

The most common offloading and loading of shipping containers is a tilt bed trailer which can slide your container off. First, you have to prepare your foundation and employ the services of a skilled driver to move your container right on the foundation. if your foundation is not ready as of the time of delivery, you will need to look at other options.

If your site is not well cleared, you need to strategize how you will carefully navigate through with your vehicle and equipment. It could be a bigger deal when more than one container is involved. Hence, you need to plan your vehicle navigation with the help of a contractor.

1. Tilt bed slide off: This vehicle is known to have a hydraulically-actuated tilt bed that can slide your container on top of the ground without much hassles. Once the container begins to slide down, friction would move it until it lands on the ground. The front side of the container is to land first before the other parts finally rest on the ground.

There are certain things you need to consider when using a tilt bed slide off:

- Ground surface: the container would have to be positioned in a way that it is backing the grounds upon which the container will be placed. Hence, the driveway needs to be flat and smooth. This loading option is most suitable for slab or piers foundations.
- Overhead clearance: the container will be raised to 20 feet or more before it finally settles down, hence there must be no overhead structures in place.
- Front clearance: there must be no obstruction at least within 40-feets or more of the foundation especially if you are delivering with a large truck. The truck would need a lot of space to navigate and maneuver before, during and after loading.
- Vertical stacking: you cannot stack vertically with the tilt bed slide off because this equipment can't place container on container, you would need to hire another equipment to handle this for you.

2. Side loader: This truck has a side-loading device that enables the truck to load the container through its side straight on your foundation. Things to consider:
- Ground surface: these trucks must have long sides that possess hydraulic outriggers that prevent the container from tipping off. these outriggers might take a lot of space in the truck so make enough room for them.
- Overhead clearance: the side loader would release the container slightly before offloading it, so make sure there are no structural obstructions at the top.
- Vertical stacking: side loaders can only stack two containers at a time due to the presence of outriggers.
3. Forklift: The forklift used here is a higher model that can be used to handle weight. This forklift is usually a rough terrain model. However, it is usually separate from the truck so you have to bring it to your site through another way. Types;
- Piggyback: these are forklifts made to be attached to the back of the trailer with their forks. The

forklifts that are used with this equipment can only hold a 2ft container.
- Separately trucked: this is the next direct alternative for a piggyback.

Things to consider:

- Ground surface: the truck can be parked anywhere close to the foundation because the forklift cannot stretch so much. However, obstructions like ruts, hills or metals will cause a challenge when the forklift is about to offload the container.
- Overhead clearance: a forklift is quite manipulative; it can function well irrespective of the obstructions.
- Weight: the largest model of forklift can carry a 40ft container. A loaded container is heavier and might be difficult for the forklift to carry.
- Vertical stacking: different forklift models have different stacking abilities. Some can stack one or two containers on top of a base container. Stacking with a forklift is easier when the ground is even and flat.

4. Traditional crane: This is another common offloading container lifter. They allow for flexible movement of containers but they are quite expensive to manage especially if you stay in a rural area. It could be hard to get a crane to be parked on your site and help you lift your container. This option is not cost-effective with only one container. It is best for moving more than one container at a time.

Things to consider:

- Ground surface: the crane is the only option that allows you to place the container on uneven terrain without causing hazards. However, it needs to be parked on flat ground to function properly.
- Overhead clearance: the crane is a very large vehicle and cannot function amid any obstruction, make sure that all obstructions are distanced as much as possible.
- Weight: generally, there are different categories of crane weights. However, cranes can carry any type of shipping container, full or empty. The

horizontal distance between the crane and the container is what matters most.
- Vertical stacking: cranes give you a variety of stacking options. You can stack as many containers as you want with a traditional crane.
5. Truck-mounted crane: This crane is very different from a regular crane in that it allows for you to transport a 20ft container without having to separate the crane from the container. The crane is much smaller than the regular crane, therefore a lot of functions are reduced.

Things to consider:

- Ground surface: this crane is smaller than other trucks and will need to be parked close to the container site.
- Overhead clearance: the same situation applies to a traditional crane applies here.
- Weight: most truck-mounted cranes cannot carry a full container; they can only carry 20ft container. The weight is usually measured by the weight of the container plus the distance of the container from the crane.

- Vertical stacking: you will need to speak with the operator to check if the vertical stacking can be done with cranes and accommodating short-level stacks.
6. Hydraulic lifting jack: This is one very interesting method for offloading containers. In this machine, the hydraulic legs move from the trailer so the container moves off the trailer and slowly lowers to the ground as the trailer begins to drive away. This method doesn't require the container to move on the horizontal scale, the container just tends to go straight to the ground.

Things to consider:

- Ground surface: a level surface is very important for the truck to achieve a smooth approach.
- Overhead clearance: the container has to be raised a little above the truck for it to drop so it is not really affected by overhead obstructions.
- Weight: irrespective of the model, the jacks need to be checked constantly. It might have issues with a loaded container. An empty container is usually easy to lift.
- Vertical stacking: it cannot stack containers.

7. Machine lifting jack: This jack is very much in similitude with the hydraulic lifting jack. However, it isn't powered by any force. You have to manually join the chain hoist and lift or lower the container to make it move. It is a simpler alternative to the hydraulic option, the only downside is that it is very much slower. If you intend to move just one container, it is a good option to consider.

Things to consider:

The considerations are the same with the hydraulic lifting jacks.

Chapter 8

Installation of Utilities

Utilities are necessities that you cannot afford to do without on your building site. You don't just need them in your container when you must have finished building, they would also help you to make building easy. There are companies responsible for servicing utilities in different locations, you can do an online search to find the ones servicing your building location. Before striking a deal, ensure you understand the rates and terms of payment. Some utilities involve minimum monthly charges. These charges start to count after installation. So might consider waiting to commence building before installing these utilities.

Some of these utilities are regulated by the government which is much more affordable. Endeavor to do your research well before settling for a utility company.

Electricity

This is one of the most essential utilities that you cannot do without even at construction. Contact an electrical company to get familiar with the processes required in setting up an electricity meter. If there is a power line across your road, it is much easier to get power installed into your container building. The cost is most times dependent on if there will be the need to buy a transformer for your container, the difficulty of the installation process, the installation location (poles or underground).

The utility company usually provides a short length of poles and wire, if you want to use it for a longer distance, you'll need to pay for extra wire. You should get an estimate for the extra amount of wire you'll be using. You might get a discount on your first month's service fee. Another issue that you might have is that some electrical companies might desire that your building attains some form of progress before they install electrical appliances in it. They might have reservations about the possibility of you finding the building and maintaining a beneficial customer relationship with them. This is not so with every company, so do your research well to understand the company's policies before you sign up for anything. You might have to start your building on temporary power, at least it would provide you short electrical circuits. You can use it for construction but it might be too small to power your appliances after building. After construction, you can ask for permanent service.

Gas

This is mostly used in space heating, for water heaters and stoves. It basically includes natural gas or propane. If you are building in the city, you can contact a gas distributor just the same way an electrical service agent works. If you are not close to the city, you can purchase a heavy tank that contains gas that can last for a month time or longer. However, endeavor to find the cost of gas in your location before going to make a decision.

Sewer and Septic

Different sewer lines have different policies and processes for tying in, you need to do your research to familiarize yourself with these processes before settling for an option. A septic line is best for rural areas. The setup is always costlier than a sewer system but after installation, it requires no cost for usage. Unlike the sewer system where you have to consistently pay to use. Septic tanks are usually buried with lines or pipes. You are to discuss and strategize with your contractor and installer on a location that won't disturb your construction process at the moment or in the future.

Telecommunication

If communication and connectivity are vital to you, there are various options you can consider to make sure you stay connected and have access to constant communication with your loved ones around the world.

There are several options available which spans from DSL, cable, fiber, and others that influence the television network services, internet, and phone connectivity. In rural locations, you might need to use slower speed cable, satellite dishes, DSL connections and point-to-point radio frequency techniques. If you live in a location that allows you to have access to multiple options, do well to compare pricing rates, and availability to prevent haggling and poor network connectivity. You can make a better decision by consulting people living around there to know what they use and how they use it. Making sure you have active telecommunication services at an early point is highly necessary to aid google tracking of stores, and the installation of a security camera.

Water

Some developed states like the United States have provisions for neat water, their water is neat enough to serve you for bathing, laundry and cooking. However, in some other underdeveloped locations, you might need to make separate provisions for your drinking water, probably a portable plastic water can. Rural areas also have their provision for water supply, although it could be very stressful or difficult to access. You have the option of digging a well, a borehole or commissioning a water distribution company to fill your water tank periodically. Some of these options might have high upfront costs but is most profitable in the long run and is more hygienic.

A Short message from the Author:

Hey, I hope you are enjoying the book? I would love to hear your thoughts!

Many readers do not know how hard reviews are to come by and how much they help an author.

I would be incredibly grateful if you could take just 60 seconds to write a short review on Amazon, even if it is a few sentences!

\>\> Click here to leave a quick review

Thanks for the time taken to share your thoughts!

Chapter 9

Roofing The Container

Deciding on adding a roof to your container is not a big deal, this decision is made dependent on your building design and the required cost against your budget. Many persons shy from roofing their container homes because of the extra cost; however, they lose the extra insulation benefits and decrease in energy bills roofing provides. With a roof, you can easily insulate inside the container and reduce the heat temperature, the roof will be a passage for the hot air to disseminate. A roof also helps to provide a good roof bar above your windows and doors to prevent the unpleasant occurrence of rain dripping through the windows and doors.

Roof Styles

Shed

This is a sloped style of roof. It is very easy to build, with the right tool, you can make this yourself and install it in just a few days. Sheds also give you the alternative of using solar panels, you can position yourself on one of the long sides. When planning on installing a shed, weld the steel plates at a right angle on both sides of the container. Use your nails to attach the steel plates to wooden beams. After screwing or nailing it firmly, the slope begins to form. Screw-in steel bars just across the trusses to help secure your roof's structure and. Your steel bar should be measured about 20 foot and your trusses must be well braced to prevent the wind from blowing into your space.

At this stage, your structural engineer would have to state the remaining specifications and guide you through them. These specifications would include estimations such as the load-bearing requirements for your roof. There are different estimations in different regions. The load-bearing requirements are very necessary because it determines the ability of a roof to withstand forces like rain, sunshine, and snowy falls. Covering your roof would require you to make use of galvanized metal and coated sheets. The most durable is proven to be coated sheets because it is shield by strong chemicals and properties. The galvanized sheets are easier to fix but not as durable. Finally, before calling this a wrap, you need to make provision for adequate ventilation. Lift your trusses a lit higher to make it hang over the container and position a fascia just below it. The fascia or soffit board must have an inch air gap in between it that is well covered with wire mesh to allow airflow through the roof. To enhance the ventilation, cut off the slots from the steel with a disc cutter to prevent condensation and heat traps that could cause rust.

Gable

The next viable roof alternative is the gable-styled roof. This is the most common roof used in a traditional home, so if you will want your home to look more traditional, you can use this roof. It has a triangular hut-like shape. The slope caused by the triangle helps to provide good water drainage. Gabled roofs are known to last long without rusting or having leaks. It also allows for more ceiling space which is helpful in insulation, than other roof types. This roof is constructed in similar stages with the shed roof.

Weld the steel plates over the sides of the shipping container to install a gable-style roof. The respective sides of the container should be attached to a wooden beam. This beam should be screwed into the trusses and the steel should be adjusted so the roof's shape begins to take place. screw in your purlins over the trusses to make the roof's structure complete. Use shingles or coated sheets to do your finishing. The truss should be placed over the container and a soffit board should be screwed in below the trusses. The fascia or soffit board must have an inch air gap in between it that is well covered with wire mesh to allow airflow through the roof

Flat

This is the conceptional roof that comes with the container. It could be good enough for some building structures. However, it has the general disadvantage of sustaining water in pools over the roof. Many persons use it because it is a much cheaper option and it doesn't require you to make any long installation plans and preparations. However, the flat roof requires some extra installations that make it safer and more convenient to use. You can overlay a thick tarpaulin sheet and position rolls of asphalt on it. It will reduce the dampness caused by rain or winter on the roof.

Why You Need a Structural Engineer?

Irrespective of the roof type you select, it is very expedient that you work hand-in-hand with professional personnel when building, preferably a structural engineer to guide you through the process and make correct estimations/ specifications as regards measurements. Basically, they help you to decide your roof's load-bearing requirements. This is estimated by calculating the transient load, dead, or live load of the roof.

- Dead load refers to the total weight of all the building materials used in setting up the roof.
- Live load is the estimated weight of the people and the tools they use in installing the roof.
- Transient load is the estimated stresses caused by natural factors like wind, snow and rain on the roof.

The total weight of your roof is the sum of all these estimates. It is also the capacity of your roof to maintain structure without falling or wearing out. Every district or region has spelled out load requirements for building a roof because every area has its different weather challenges or building constraints. Some locations are prone to long strong winds, heavy rainfalls, and tough snows. Places like this will require that the roof be established with extra bracing for the trusses. Finally, irrespective of the roof type you select, do well to prioritize ventilation to avoid condensation or rusting.

Chapter 10

Container Flooring

Inspecting The Original Floors of The Container

The hardwoods in shipping containers are laminated from teak woods, and they are structured under marine requirements to make them durable and tough enough to withstand salty waters. Also, they are sterilized or treated with chemical treatment in accordance with the import/ export regulations. Some of these floorings are known to inhabit viruses and contaminants. You are to ensure you discard them before beginning any work on your container interior. You would be able to escape this dilemma if you purchase new containers because it has not been used and it is void of contaminants. You could still indicate your preference for an alternative flooring type when ordering a used shipping container.

Considering, the extra cost of flooring your container, you might decide to retain the original container floor. However, you have to ensure that it is safe and free of hazardous chemicals. You can check the chemical type used in flooring on the safe convention plate that is usually screwed to the front of the container. This plate contains three individual sections; the treatment date, chemical type, and immunity. You can discover how safe or hazardous it is from this information.

Here are things to check out for when inspecting the original floors of the container. Usually, basic information is on the safe convention plate but there is always an exception of some categories of information. Some of the hidden information might include;

- Was there any damage to the flooring at any time?
- Was the damage replaced?
- What type of products was the container shipping?
- Did the chemical spill off on the floor in the process of transportation?

This information is majorly concealed by the supplier. Hence, you have to be sure that you're dealing with a trustworthy supplier, that's the only way you can figure out these answers.

However, you could still conduct your own individual check and validate the safety of your container floors.

If you are unfamiliar with the container safe convention plate information, you might not understand most of the information there when inspecting your container floors. On that plate, there is a section titled timber component treatment. It has the following details under it;

- Immunity (IM)
- Chemical used in treating the floor
- Date of chemical treatment.

To identify harmful chemicals, check out the list provided by the WHO pesticide classification guide so you can understand the risk that each pesticide type includes. This plate is usually changed upon every treatment of the floor. So, you can trust that the information is updated and valid.

Asides from the safety of the flooring, you need to also check the structural accuracy and perfection of the container floors. All these decisions must be made before you start working on your container interiors because this is much more affordable.

Remove or Not Remove the Original Floor?

Although, cost could be a deterring factor in deciding what to do with your container floors. It is almost expected that you change the floors. Because a new floor is more durable and gives your building an aesthetic look. No matter how durable your container floor is you need to still consider removing it to place a new one. If you decide to still keep the original container floor, you need to epoxy it. Epoxy is a commercial way of sealing your container home floor. It will give it a whole new look entirely and increase its longevity. However, epoxy is quite toxic and would need to be handled with a respirator or full ventilation to reduce its toxicity. Do well to clean your plywood with a chemical preferably an isopropyl alcohol to give you the best bond.

Removing the Original Floor

Removing a container floor starts from cutting open holes around the place where there are bolts to easily remove it from the bolt. You can use a simple saw or a hand drill for a more perfect effect. After sawing, what is left is to pull out the wood. This could prove to be difficult in older shipping containers because over the years, it has built tension and it is more difficult to pull out wood from the container. However, a medium-sized screw bar is a strong enough tool to put into work at this point.

If this proves to be quite stressful, consider cutting the wood into smaller bits and pulling every other part of the container floor that way. This is time-consuming but very effective.

Container Floor Replacement

If you have decided on removing and replacing the floors of your shipping container, there are other options you might like to consider that would give your container home a much homely feeling that you desire.

Shipping containers are cost-effective and convenient building alternatives. It is unique and conventional because the building space was formerly an industrial environment. Hence, they mostly come with hardwoods that are pumped up with harmful pesticides. The best alternative still remains to get an ideal floor type that is safe, suitable and beautiful for your container home. This way you can comfortably enjoy the small space that is now a vibrant building you can live in without many hazards. If you would be living in the container, you would have to get rid of this floor for a better, safer one. There are various options open to you, but what is the best option for you? A few of these unique floor options have been listed for you.

Best Flooring for Flat Pack Shipping Container

- Bamboo flooring: this is the most affordable, flexible, and durable replacement option for flooring your container. There is no need to cut the bamboo or remodify it into new shapes before fixing them into the container, the flooring dimensions are just the same as plywood floorings.

- Carpet flooring: if the container floor is not too toxic, you can retain it for use and look for an alternative for covering the surface so as to give your container a more aesthetic look. The carpet is a better covering option. This is the nice flexible and container flooring option; you can use different designs and colors in recreating a great look container home.

- Steel flooring: most containers come with steel flooring and a nonslip feature. You place this steel on the original plywood flooring in the container. It is stronger, durable and more water-resistant.

- Vinyl flooring: vinyl are known to be a long-lasting flooring option; they commonly last for more than one decade before you could start noticing signs of wear. It is highly resistant to scratches, rusts, and stains. A good option, if you are intending to move in with children.

- Linoleum flooring: this final option is an eco-friendly and highly durable replacement option for flooring your container. With a natural antibacterial component, it has a natural biodegradable ability that enables it to last for 40 years and more.

Chapter 11

Constructing A Wall Inside The Container

Building a wall inside the container is necessary to partition rooms and divide spaces. There are three main steps in constructing a wall, they are all discussed below;

Framing: Framing is a whole lot beyond placing coat on the walls. In framing, you need to take cognizance and due note of the electrical wiring, insulation plans and power outlets. This is termed corrugation insert. You cannot do this yourself; you will definitely need to hire an expert or professional to help you through the corrugation. The inserts usually are well-shaped wood segments that close in air gaps in the container. The bends of the container walls can be made to look flat before the inserts. After making the inserts, you have to start framing the walls. It is at this point that you get to hook the paneling. Frames need to be added inside the wall to support its stability. However, you might decide to leave out the frame until you are done with insulation because you would definitely have a lot of drilling to do during insulation.

Framing materials:

- Steel strips: this is a slim metal type used in welding inside the container. This framing option is best in areas prone to heavy rain, humidity and spread of bugs. Steels prove to be justifiable options for areas with a harsh climate.

- Wood:

The woods are usually measured in 2"×2" and wedged in with tiny nails. For a firmer effect, Duritan is used as glue to hold the wood to the container.

- Aluminum strips:

This is a combination of aluminum and metal strips. They are usually placed together, hence it is way easier to install the board after all.

Insulation: after the framing posts have been installed, you have to put in all the insulation materials. Insulation is very much necessary and mandatory because without insulation the shipping container cannot be comfortable for use. The insulation helps to put out all the harsh temperatures and keep the temperature from extreme cold and harsh heat. The weather is not consistent, it is never the same everywhere all the time of the year, you need to select an insulation type that best suits your goal. Examples of insulation include:

- Fireglass insulation: this insulation is known for its quality and thickness which is estimated at 3 ½

inches. Its insulation value is said to be good and has a value of R-13. The fiberglass panels can make the container water-resistant. Hence, it is the most commonly used insulation type. It is made with heated sand and grinded glass that is divided into tiny fibers. It is also the cheapest type of insulation in the US.
- Polystyrene foam insulation: this insulation is mostly used on plywood and it poses an insulation value of R-5. It has a 1-inch thickness. It can also be called expanded polystyrene foam (XPS). XPS is a material that is molten and pressed together into a closed-cell foam. It is usually attached with studs or glue to the body of the container.
- Closed cell foam insulation: this insulation option offers the highest value of insulation of R-6 per inch. It is mostly used to cover the corrugated part of the container. It has a tough texture that prevents any form of moisture condensation. The moisture and presence of gas help to increase its R-value.
- Thermal insulation: this is an electrical insulation method that warms up the room with machines.

The machines can be regulated to suit the required cool of the moment. It allows for flexibility and ensures that the container is safe and has a stable atmosphere irrespective of the climatic condition.

For deeper insight on insulation, kindly refer to chapter 6 where we discussed the different insulation types for your container home.

Wall Paneling: the next step after insulation is paneling. This is very important so that no cables are exposed or unnecessary spaces are available. The wall should be perfectly covered and well coated. This is the last technical work before painting and polishing. The available paneling option is dependent on the use of your shipping container.

- Dry wall option: this is a mud-like finishing. It is quite smooth and has nice polishing. It is best used for finishing permanent structures.

- Sandalwood: this option gives you a clean finish without any form of damage to the wall. The appearance is very sleek, smooth and clean.

- Plywood: the finishing is rough which makes it most suitable for workshops or a storage unit. The rough texture makes it unfitting for an office space, bedroom, or living room even after coating.

- Fiberglass: this is usually used in synchronization with the plywood. The fiber glass is used to cover the rough texture of the plywood with white plastic. The most interesting part of this wall option is that it is washable and it is water-resistant.

- Aluminum and steel: this is mainly used on the container's exterior. It has a very smooth coating and it is insulated with seams that happen to be quite visible in the wall. It is also easy to clean and wash. However, it is the most expensive wall type.

- Perforated steel sheets: this is a higher quality of steel paneling. The walls are well insulated with seams and foams, which are covered fully with a quiet feel. It is easy to move from one point to another but it is also expensive.

Chapter 12

Door and Window Installation

Doors and windows are a necessity for constructing a building for access and ambiance. However, the construction of doors and windows in a shipping container is much different. Below, we will discuss the 9 steps involved in the installation of doors and windows in shipping containers.

Selecting the type of doors, windows and their frames:

There are different types and sizes of windows and doors. The style and size of a door and window will determine its mode of installation. Shipping containers are usually built with corten steel. Hence, they react differently from others. Using aluminum on steel could result in galvanic corrosion, that is the steel begins to corrode. However, when the aluminum is painted, there is a separation between the dissimilar metals from corrosion. Steel screws could also help to separate raw aluminum from raw steel.

A door and window made with wood or steel could save you the stress of trying to bypass galvanic corrosion. Your walls are thick based on the weight and size of insulation that you insert in it, as well as the stud sizes, and exterior elements. You cannot install a frame that is bigger than your wall size and thickness. You are to frame your wall with equivalent thickness for your windows and doors.

Select the type and size of metal framing to install:

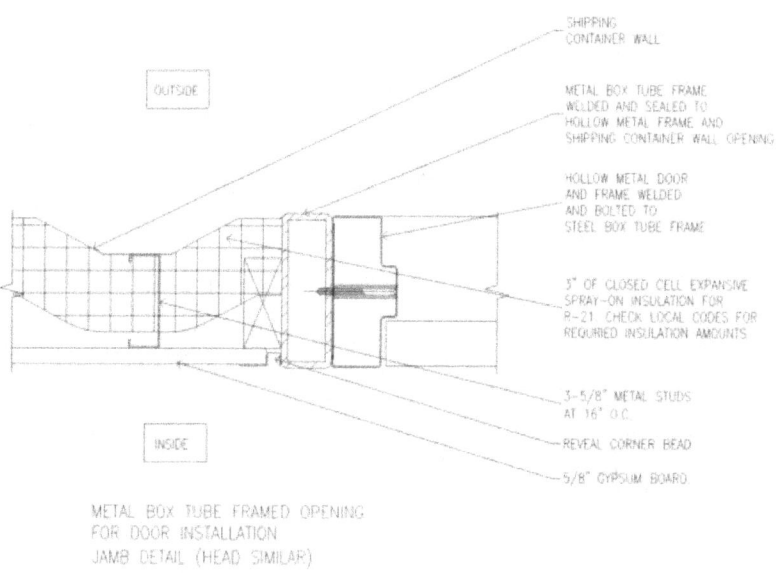

METAL BOX TUBE FRAMED OPENING
FOR DOOR INSTALLATION
JAMB DETAIL (HEAD SIMILAR)

You would need to hire the services of a professional builder or architect to check out the tube angle for framing your door and windows. The amount of load placed on the depth of the wall needs to be considered in order to determine the right size for the steel angle for framing the opening. This section usually comes in a box frame and it is structured with a steel tube. Most builders do use steel angles. Below are some advantages and disadvantages of using tube steel

- Tube steels make provision for a complete and continuous surface area which is usually from the exterior front to the full in-depth of the finished wall. The depth of the wall frame should determine the depth of your door. Hence, it is much easier to fix frames for doors and windows without having to put in studs at the round opening.
- Cutting out this opening can be quite stressful because of the corrugation of the container walls. If not done with precision, this opening might end up being poorly cut out and the square shape would not be achieved. You might be able to fix this with a bead of weld. The cut might happen to be too rough for fixing in a bead of weld, this could be a problem.

- Also, the beading with weld can get worse and start to allow for water passage, especially in hot and sunny environments.

Here are the advantages and disadvantages of using steel angles for framing doors and windows;

- To install a steel angle, you need to place the back leg of the angle in the shipping container and let the other leg stick outside. This will help to cut out any form of irregularities encountered across opening the door because the back leg stands as overlap for the gaps. Hence, the opening is tight and weather resistant. The seal is strong and firm. This tightness is greatly reliant on the overlapping metals. Nonetheless, there is no sufficient space for a door or window to be installed against. Hence, studs will be positioned inside the shipping container to fit the depth of the tube steel frame.
- Cutting and welding the metal frame to the size of the new door and window frames: placing the actual window or door frame on the site before installation will help you to figure out what measurement of angle or tube needs to be made

for the installation of the door and window. The dimensions of the inside and outside of the container must be fitting hence measurement must be taken accurately. After taking the measurements also ensure to make an allowance in measurement for the installation of the metal frames. After the doors and windows have been fixed, any extra space can be closed up with sealants. You would need to make provision for temporary support during installation to hold up the windows and doors of the frame until they are permanently and firmly fixed. The frames can bend and shift if not properly held or aligned. When this happens, irrespective of your other circumspection and carefulness, your door will fail to fit into the door frame opening.

Mark out the shipping container is to be cut for the new framing for the door and windows:

This rule is very compulsory to keep a door frame fixed perfectly into a container. It will also help you to make accurate cuttings for the box frame on the container. Get a ¼" thick × 3"×6" steel support plate and weld them at the bottom of the shipping container. These plates are to be placed at the bottom of the vertical ends of the box section frame location. This will help to hold up the frame when the box opening is being traced in the container walls. A piece of pencil or marker can be used to mark out the cut line. Make the mark a little longer than 1/16" of the box frame size on the container wall. After the opening has been marked, bring down your temporary support and grind the remaining steel surfaces until it is smooth.

Cut the new door and windows openings:

Now the dirty work has been, cut from the bottom and the sides until the whole corner is out. After the cut, position two 2×4's in the opening. The bottom is to be placed on the ground and the tops should be nicking the top of the container. Before you cut from the top and put the whole corner out, ensure that the cutting at the sides and bottom is perfect then cut the top out. Be careful when making this cut because the metal could fall inside or outside the container, no one should hang around the work area at this point. This cut should be made with a hand grinder.

Weld the metal frame on the shipping container at the cut opening:

Make sure your walls are still sleek and straight and no part has bowed out yet. If there is any abnormality, you might need to fix it with a weld. Weld in some tiny hooks to fit into the space and fix the issue. You can also weld a stiffener to straighten the bow. Fix the frame into the opening in the container space using tack welds. Make these welds on all the sides and the top or bottom corners of the container. Thereafter, place a weld on the top of the frame of about 4" long. The weld should be about 1" and should be welded at 10 degrees on all the sides of the frame.

Install the door and windows into the metal frame:

There are different alternatives for installing your windows and doors. You can make use of neoprene washers, wood blocking, and plastic separators to separate the materials that are not similar. Surfaces that are painted might have less corrosion. Also, the screw holes should be painted to reduce the corrosion they are exposed to because screw holes could be exposed to corrosion if they don't have paint on them. connectors like steel screws will also limit the exposure to corrosion. Most shipping containers were not built with screws and attachments, the manufacturer used construction adhesives and applied force in ensuring the door frames and the container doors are well-fitting against each other. This adhesives method of installation helps to reduce the number of openings and its result on the container. Too many openings could lead to water infiltrations and corrosion. It is the best method of fixing doors if you can get access to them. It is much better than fasteners.

Place a seal around the door and windows:

You need to close up all exposed gaps with beads of sealant. Take your time to carefully select a finish that will be fitting to the finishing of your building. There are various colors of sealants. If the sealants you choose are not the same as your interior finishing you can paint it with a good paint coat. You can apply paint on it as you paint other parts of the frames and the walls.

Install interior and exterior finishes around the doors and windows:

There are many variations of finishes for installing doors and windows. Your doors and windows should be befitting your chosen interior and exterior finishing. The interior finish must be the same as the color of the window frame and the interior part of the door. You have to determine the depth of your frame (box or angle section) first before preparing the finishing of the doors and windows. To install the exterior finishes, there should be a layer of flashing in between the surface of the container and the finishing. Make provisions for barriers to reduce water contact with the shipping container exterior walls. The exterior finishes will determine the way you finish the door and window frames. Most builders use wood, PVC and metal trim around the openings of the doors and windows. You can create a trim to hide peculiar irregularities where two different finishes are made.

Safety concerns when installing a window and door:

Installation involves the use of tough and dangerous power tools most times and you might have to move them from one point to another. You would also have persons around you while you are making this movement. Hence, the need to be careful and precautious. It is best and safer not to work alone. Have an assistant with you on-site that can help you hold during installations, measurements, finishing and all forms of necessary modifications. Ensure that everyone on the site is also safe and protected against possible dangers.

Chapter 13

Finalizing The Exterior

Container homes are known for their architectural flexibility and aesthetic potentiality. With the right inspirations and the right materials, container homes are now customized modern houses. Asides from aesthetic purposes, container homes are also designed for functionality purposes. The outdoor finishing is intended to keep water from affecting the container and other purposes. Cladding is one of the techniques used in covering up containers with materials to give them a whole new look. Most of the materials used are traditional and are cost-effective. Some of these materials are really expensive and would involve distinctive styling to keep them in perfect shape. Note that your exterior should be clad with breathable materials. There should not be so much covering to prevent the container from breathing. In selecting your exterior materials, note the cost, R-factor, durability, and required maintenance.

Cladding Materials

Timbre

Timbre is one of the oldest building materials before traditional houses became a thing. It has not still lost its relevance today as many people still use this material in cladding their containers after construction. When painted or stained, the timbre is a perfect material for giving quality aesthetics building design. Timbre are materials of elegance. You can make them blend with any background color while still maintaining their rustic look. What more? Timbre is eco-friendly and its woods have a unique feel it gives a colorless and lifeless construction like the container home.

There are two basic types of wood; softwood and hardwood.

Under the softwood category, there is redwood, red cedar; and the hardwood category includes oakwood, chestnut, and larch. All these woods have tannins which is a repellant for decays and rot. Most especially the hardwood, they are firmer, more water-resistant, and pest intolerant. You can get these woods in various appealing colors. However, harsh weather conditions could cause these colors to deplete. This is why it is advised that you paint them to ensure the color stays longer and you retain their warmness. You might have to re-coat every 3-5 years interval. Also, note that timbers are highly flammable and could cause health hazards when exposed to burning or fire. Timber when converted for exterior cladding purposes can be modified to boards, half-logs, shingles, and many others. You can use any of these modifications to create great aesthetic effects. Timber is also a great insulation material and proves to be most fitting for container homes.

Out of all the listed types of woods, cedar is the most appealing. It has natural captivating beauty, a variety of colors, and a beautiful aroma. It also has high resistance to rot, insects and moisture. Although it is the most expensive of the rest, it can last outdoor for years without treatment. However, in a long time, it could give way to natural effects because every wood has biodegradable features. You might need to treat it after a few years or change it totally.

The most popular means of protecting timber is coating. Stains are better coating options because it allows the color to go right into the fibers of the wood. stains last longer and do not peel off like paints.

Different versions of stain:

1. Surface stains: these stains are best for vertical coating, and it provides a great UV protection. Also, it provides a solid breathable adhesion to wood fibers. It is also water-resistant.

2. Hybrid stains: it can penetrate the deepest shallow of woods and provides very tough UV protection. It is partially breathable but tends to

leave out films on the surface that might crack or peel.

3. Deep-penetrating stains: they are impermeable by water and are not breathable. They also have UV protection but their tolerance is very poor. The colors quickly fade, and it might crack and peel on the surface.

Bamboo

This is a fast-growing tree and an eco-friendly material for exterior cladding. In 4-6 years, you can harvest giant bamboo stems in very fertile grounds. There is no need for deforestation after harvest because the stems would grow out of new bamboos after being cut down. These are great cladding materials as they also have their own aesthetic look they give to a container but can lose their color after long years of being exposed to moisture. Also, they are very durable but when coated, the coating can easily wear off or go faint. You can take them through a steaming process to make them stronger and better materials. The woods are usually split along the length, and the outer skin is peeled off to treat the wood and give it a natural brownish look. You can then join these individual woods to form solid boards for exterior cladding. Even without chemical effects, they could withstand fire, unlike natural woods. They are also eco-friendly and fast-growing.

After treating or steaming the bamboo, they tend to keep their original color, especially after being sealed by oil. They become tough, durable, and weather durable. The only disadvantage is that due to deforestation, bamboos are quite hard to find. Some companies focus on the modification and engineering of bamboo for exterior cladding, you can get your own from them. they also offer a clip & lock system in place for nailing and attachments which makes installation a lot easier.

Engineered Wood

Woods can be engineered to preserve the natural aesthetic properties of wood and increase its durability and water resistance capability. Engineering wood is termed as Wood Plastic Composite. It contains 50% of powdered wood fiber, 35-40% of HDPE plastic and 10-15% of other additives. HDPE is health hazard-free and approved by the food industry. There might be off-gassing, but it is not usually the main effect. Engineering woods give you a feel of the two different worlds, the natural and the WPC boards. These boards are nontoxic and depend mostly on the recipe of manufacturers. WPC is strong, water-resistant, and fireproof. It comes in various colors, styles, shapes, and textures. You can flex it into whatever wood texture you want. However, it cannot be painted frequently, it doesn't require maintenance at all. The way they come is the way you get to use them till you decide to recycle.

Fiber-Cement Boards

These boards are made from concrete and cellulose fibers plus certain additives. Concretes make up 60% of the total volume and the fibers which are used in reinforcing the concrete are about 10%. Usually, they come with cenospheres which are usually lightweight and hollow spheres of silica and alumina of 30%. They help to make even the weight and density of fiber-cement boards. Generally, after the composition has been thoroughly mixed, the cement fiber turns out to be an environmentally friendly option. They are also UV tolerant, weather-resistant and fireproof. They come in different shapes and finishes from smooth to vibrant. They can be made to imitate other wood types like timber. If carefully and excellently done, there could be only little clues to different it from timber. However, fiber cement boards are expensive to make as it involves the composition of many materials. Although it is usually painted before installation, you can still repaint it afterward to make them attractive. Fiber-cement boards tend to retain a gray appearance when uncoated. In such forms, they are easily penetrable by vapor and moisture. When exposed to weather, the surface can become porous and there will be permanent deformation. Effluence might also take place. it is very necessary that the cladding is sealed after installation to prevent exposure to moisture. You could also use the Tyvek- moisture barrier and install it behind the wood as a protective substance.

Fiber-cement boards are installed with tongue or groove systems. It cannot be used as an extra insulation value to the container because it has a low R-value. Also, the acoustic and thermal insulation are made to go together.

Composite Materials

These are combinations of two separate substances to create a better substance. This is stronger than the independent materials alone. Many synthetic composite materials can be combined to make a strong composite material and give firmness to the container home. Materials like this can be used anywhere and everywhere.

Composite materials are tough, weather-resistant, lightweight, corrosion, rot, mold, staining resistance, flexibility, low maintenance and durability which makes them most suitable for exterior claddings. However, they are quite expensive, non-biodegradable, and not eco-friendly. These materials are great for use despite these limitations and they can be made to match the appearance of natural cladding materials.

Composite Panels

These are made of materials from between laminated metal sheets also referred to as Sandwich panels. They can be used for the interior layer of insulation, exterior siding and cladding. They are mostly used on building load-bearing walls because of their toughness and firmness. They have the same corrugated likeness of the container and can be made to suit the containers perfectly. There are different materials like mineral wool, polystyrene foams, and fiberglass. These metal sheets are also clothes with polyvinyl chloride, polyvinylidene fluoride (PVDF), acrylic paints, silicone polyester. Composite panels are weather-resistant, insect resistant and do not need any maintenance. Their colors last for very long years before starting to fade. However, the panels are made to mimic the woods which is not workable and could be quite expensive.

Metal

Putting metal as an exterior cladding over a metal container might sound absurd but has its unique merits. One of which is that it allows you to install an exterior thermal insulation and preserving the weather-related benefits of the metal envelope. Metal cladding is highly beneficial because it is fire-resistant, water-resistant, durable, strong and offers UV protection. The maintenance required for metal cladding is bordered about washing, painting, and checking for corrosion. Metal claddings are made from aluminum, zinc, stainless steel, brass, copper as against containers that are made with COR-Ten-Steel. When painted, copper alloys are complimented for their characteristic greenish patina and they could be extra expensive. Corten steel might become rusty along the line and develop layers of firm coating which might be firm enough to prevent corrosion. In areas with a terrible climate, corrosion might be unavoidable. Metal also can transfer heat and give a smooth aesthetic surface for coating. You can make different styles and forms of cladding with metal, also there is a large pallet of colors you can use.

Cladding Installation

Inserting installation during cladding might be a challenge, you need to ensure that you are not trivializing any of the insulation materials. There are different ways of installation, most people use metal screws because it is firm and long-lasting. However, it will require that you make holes in the wall which could jeopardize the entire process by reducing the airtightness. You might need to build a support for the installation of your exterior clads. You need to apply glue to the wood to get the wood to stick to the body of the container. The corrugated walls have metal screws that ensure safety. It depends on your time and the available resources.

Cladding Only: this is when you apply the external cladding for aesthetic reasons. This makes the task quite easy. You don't have to screw open the walls and cause infiltration of air.

Cladding With Exterior Insulation: cladding with exterior insulation could be complex because you'll have to make it tight enough to prevent air infiltrations through the cladding. You want it to stay airtight knowing that any contact with water could destroy your insulation. The best insulation to use is closed-cell spray foam insulation. You can simply attach them to your walls and they are thick and hard. In heavy rainy periods, they might be affected by the moisture and develop mildew. To avoid this, get a breathable cladding that would help it dry out the moisture it had earlier gathered.

Painting the Container

Some delivery vans might offer to help paint you delivering the container. This is not necessary if you will be doing a lot of modification on the container because you'll mess up the paint in the process and need to repaint or prepare the container for a new painting. Painting is expected to happen after installations and cladding, so all the welded areas will be welded. There are varieties of colors you can use, here are a few points to note when painting your container;

- The best paint to use is the marine-grade direct-to-metal waterborne. You can select different colors under this paint type. These paint types will help you to preserve your container color. Avoid any solvent paint, it is sure to peel or fade away with time. Another good paint type is acrylic alkyd paint.

- Now that you have selected your paint type and color, wait till it's sunny before you set out to paint your container.

- Clear off rusts and corrosion areas. Pressure wash for a more effective effect. Use vinegar to clean off the remaining particles.

- Use a rust reformer to adhere the color to the container surface.

- You can use a roller or spray to apply the paint afterward. The choice is yours.

- To paint your container's interior, endeavor to allow for ventilation and wear protection over your sense organs. Do not spray on wood, and spray a rich primer before rolling or spraying the paint.

- Maintaining the container paint requires using a rust reformer to dust off any affected area. Use double coats and create multiple layers of paints.

Chapter 14

Ideas for Your Interior Design

Container homes are a whole big deal these days because people tend to use them for several reasons such as the minimalist lifestyle, part-time usage and affordability. For whatever reason you consider living in a container home, you'll not want to spare the insides and make it look like a dry ineffable shoebox. Even in the small available space, you'll want o to ensure all your properties and necessary household goods are duly accommodated like clothing and accessories. Putting all this and finding sufficient space to move about the house can be quite a challenge. Hence, you have to use what you have and structure your interiors in a way that it feels bigger so it can accommodate all of your property and still give you space to move about.

One way of making your home feel bigger is by physically increasing your available space.

The second way is by making use of special interior design ideas and tactics to effectively put to use the available space and make it appear larger than it actually is. This is termed reduced-sized housing.

Design Idea 1

Sliding Doors

When wanting to manage space, you have to be mindful of every dead space that's being caused by certain constructions or structures. The swinging door is one structure that causes a lot of dead space. There is a lot of space that goes into nothing because there is a swing door at the corner. A door of 32-inch width has over 11feet swept area. 11 feet for nothing but just a space for swing doors. Such a waste! This problem is solved by the sliding door. These doors can be slid from one endpoint to the other without taking in any extra space than the opening. There is no swept area. There are two main types of sliding doors;

Barn Doors:

This is an unconventional door that has been used for several years. It is made out of rustic wood and then modified to make it look like a barn. These doors are aesthetic in themselves and sorts of give the home a warm feel because of the nativity of the door. The only disadvantage of barn doors is that the door is held by a track mounted on the wall. This implies that when the door is open, a portion of the wall is covered by the door. Therefore, it renders that wall space useless.

Pocket Doors:

This is a more conventional sliding door. The difference between this door and the barn door is that the track that holds the door is hidden in the wall, so when the door is opened, it slides into the track in the wall. Hence, your wall area is free for use. No overstretched swept area or wall area. You can use the free walls for setting up furniture or shelves.

Design Idea 2

Convertible Couches

Technology has given us the opportunity of multitasking with furniture and household necessities. Convertible couches are an awesome way of maximizing your small space area in comfort. It is simply a piece of furniture that can serve multiple purposes when needed. An example is a convertible couch that can be used for bed and other new modifications. This furniture also helps to give your home a touch of excellence in flexibility and versatility. The convertible couch can be positioned anywhere as it can be used for multiple purposes; in the room, it can be used as a min sofa and a sleeping area. In the living room, it can serve as a long couch and a guest bed. here are some individual types of convertible couches.

Futon:

This is a Japanese traditional bedding style. This is a bed that can be folded along the length and be converted to a couch. When folded, it forms the L shape of a small sofa. When needed for sleeping, you just need to unfold and there you have your mattress.

Daybed:

The daybed is a modern bed that comes with a short headboard that stretches through one length of the bed. when converted and folded into a sofa, the board becomes a backrest. It comes in many options, commonly a narrow twin-sized mattress.

Foldout Couch/Sleeper Sofa:

This is a bed but it has the likeliness and appearance of a sofa. This is why it is called the sleeper sofa. If you want to extend the bed and make it longer for sleeping, you can remove the cushion, you will find a mattress and frame in a folded form. If you overturn it this way, you will realize that the surface you sleep on is different from the cushion's surface.

Chaise:

Chaise is short for the French word Chaise lounge which means long chair. This chair comes with extra support for you to place your leg. The backrest is short and it has a long/ extensive cushion. It is majorly used for napping. However, people of smaller body stature can still use it to get a comfortable sleep at night.

Design Idea 3

Using the Walls

Living in small/ reduced sized housing requires that you make use of every space, especially your walls. The walls are an extension of the floor space, and there is limited floor space, you can extend your equipment and storage to your walls. In a container, your walls are a great asset, this is why we have to get rid of every obstruction to using the wall. Below are examples or tips on how to make advantageous use of your wall.

Wall-Mounted Desks:

There are different fashions of wall-mounted desks. The commonest t is the floating desk. This desk is attached firmly to the wall without the necessary support from the floor or any other part of the wall. In most cases, the desk is permanently extended into the wall. This is not ideal as it could cause certain hazards. A better choice is the folding desks. The folding desk has almost as large a workspace as the floating desk but it can be folded against the wall when not in use. It is usually supported by chains from above or below. The support isn't really the focus, the focus is that the folding desk allows you to maximize your work surface area and your room space at the same time. You could still use other wall spaces above and below the folding desk for storage with shelves and others.

TV Mounts:

This is quite common, many persons use the TV mounts even in a traditional home. Tv stands are quite traditional and aesthetic, however, mounting your TV to the wall helps you to save the space that would have been committed to a box stand. TV mounts also come with provisional outlets for cables and power sockets. You can make use of an articulating mount so that you can view the TV from different angles. TV mounts can help you maximize space and save extra money for a TV stand.

Wall-Mounted Fans:

Ceiling fans are the commonest fans used by traditional homes for building a modern house and enhancing air circulation. This is not applicable in container homes where there is a very brief ceiling height, so we need to find an alternative to the ceiling fan in a container home. A viable option would have been a standing fan but that will make you lose your floor space and expose the fan cables to the floor. The most applicable fan option is to mount the fan on the wall. You'll save space and have an effective fan circulation medium.

Design Idea 4

Rooms Without Walls

The previous section is practicable only if you have rooms with walls in your container. Walls are great room partitions, however, there is a great benefit in having few walls in your space. The permanency could be a disadvantage when you have reasons to remodify. Alternative options allow for more flexibility. However, this alternative option is commonly used in official environments like offices and urban lofts. These alternative options are better ways of dividing a space or a living area without walls. It also provides other advantages like natural lighting, lower building cost, air circulation and intensive décor options. Here are some ideas you can consider;

Hanging Fabric Curtains:

This curtain is made from different materials; dark, heavy fabric and can almost block the passage of light. It usually makes sounds when closed and it looks like a stage curtain. A thin light material allows for more natural lighting.

Hanging Beaded Curtains:

These are strings arranged together in a vertical format and hanged from the roof point. It can come in a variety of colors and designs. You can make beaded curtains of images.

Folding Panel Dividers:

There are many varieties of these dividers. One common option is trifold. You can make different designs with different colors to fit your room's color texture.

Double-Sided Bookshelf:

This is a model structure that can be used to partition space. You don't necessarily need to fill it with books. You can store other necessities in it; like awards, plaques, artworks, and picture diaries. It is a multipurpose partition option.

Rotating Entertainment Center:

This is a vertical surface that can be spun around 180 degrees. You can use the background to mount your TV and wow your friends when they show up for a movie night. There are many styles; you can get your whole wall to spin or just a part of it where the TV is positioned. The beauty remains that you can view your TV from different spots.

Double-Sided Fireplace:

This is a dual face fireplace used in cold climates seasons that are expected to last for a long time. Usually, you can use it to cover the two sides of the house it is interfacing. When it is lit on any side, it warms both sides and gives the house a glorious ambiance.

Chapter 15

Shipping Container Home Mistakes to Avoid

1. Poor foundation building: your foundation is an established premise upon which your container is built. Once your foundation is faulty, your building is just a short while from being destroyed. You would have a lot of constructional problems, and peradventure you successfully build up and finish the house, you would have a lot of container home problems because the base upon which your building is standing is faulty. You need to consider the nature of the sire you are selecting to set up your foundation before you begin building. If the ground tends to sink or has a slimy texture, then you can be sure your foundation is going to be faulty and unstable no matter how well you try to set it up. Your site composition and texture go a long way to determining the stability of your foundation and your container home eventually. Also, your foundation must be built with enough strength to

carry your container to ensure even weight distribution of your container. Note that two steps container home would require more stability and structural composure than a one-step home.

2. Miscalculating the shipping container home size: through a conducted research, it was realized that some builders make an estimation of the size of a container without confirming it and others make wrong calculations of the container and eventually end themselves up with something less satisfying or pleasing. We've established that the normal shipping containers are different from the ones used in home construction. The one for home construction is usually one fit taller because the insulation fixing is estimated to take at least one foot of the container. If the container height is too small, it makes the container look like a rat hole after insulation. Getting a container with the wrong measurement will lead to a lot of unpleasant situations eventually.

3. Buying poor shipping containers: there are different types of containers that are available for

sale as has been discussed earlier. However, there is no reason why you should get a poor container. Most used containers are likely to come with one issue or the other, it is your duty to exercise due diligence in selecting the container with a good working condition and then make little repairs where necessary. A poor container would cost you one for repairs and require a lot of maintenance when it begins to wear and tear. The general container problem is rust due to condensation of saltwater and continuous usage. If you would be selecting a container with a rusted part, be ready to make cuts through those points. When using pictures for inspection it is most likely that you might fall into a situation where you don't see every part of the container. To confirm every part of the container, you need to do video coverage.

4. Not knowing zoning codes and building regulations: before you build your container home, read wide to be well informed about the building regulations and zoning codes in your area. This will help you to avoid construction

penalties and demolition penalties. You must receive a building permit before you begin construction. Get all the necessary information before you start building.

5. Not using correct insulation: climate has a significant role that it plays in selecting the right insulation that fits shipping container home. You need to stabilize your insulation settings especially against tough climatic conditions like rain. Poor insulation can cause your container insiders to rust. There are different insulation types, you need to make sure you are using the right insulation material that will be fitting for your location. Location with a very tough cold climate would require spray foam insulation. For a location with harsh temperatures, you should use an insulation option that makes the home cool. Without putting your climate into consideration, you might settle for an unfitting insulation option.

6. Cutting out many sheets of steel from containers: modification is very necessary for building but you should be careful with modifications that

require that you cut out the steel from your container. This could reduce the texture and stability of the container. In as much as, you might find it hard to avoid making cuts for usability and aesthetics, you need to be mindful of maintaining the structural composure of the container. Make sure each of your cuts is for intensive purposes and use beams to hold up the stability in areas where you cut out steel.

7. Hiring wrong container home builders: before you start building, look out for professional home builders, you can search online or ask in your neighborhood. The stability of your building depends on the quality of the building materials and the professionalism of your engineer. This point cannot be overemphasized. Ensure that your contractor has the required skills and quality experience in the technical know-how of building a container. Not every contractor knows how a container building should be set up. Your contractor must be accurate and efficient.

The end... almost!

Hey! We've made it to the final chapter of this book, and I hope you've enjoyed it so far.

If you have not done so yet, I would be incredibly thankful if you could take just a minute to leave a quick review on Amazon

Reviews are not easy to come by, and as an independent author with a little marketing budget, I rely on you, my readers, to leave a short review on Amazon.

Even if it is just a sentence or two!

So if you really enjoyed this book, please...

\>\> Click here to leave a brief review on Amazon.

I truly appreciate your effort to leave your review, as it truly makes a huge difference.

Chapter 16

Shipping Container Home FAQs

Today many people are establishing solid structures of gyms, schools, hotels, offices and houses with shipping containers. This is because it is very much durable, efficient and affordable. We have compiled in this book everything you'll need to know about building a shipping container home. Here are answers to a few questions you might have.

1. What is the difference between container houses and regular tiny houses?

People are keen on minimalist living these days and it has led to the construction of regular tiny houses and container houses. However, these two building constructions are not in any way the same. Below are a few remarkable differences between the two;

- Space comparison: unlike the tiny house which has a limited foot area, the container house can be expanded and made bigger. By joining two shipping containers, you can achieve a space double the size of a regular tiny house. a regular tiny house is about 8.5′ × 24′ in size but a container is 20ft to 40 ft in size.

- Cost comparison: the starting cost of both houses is about $40,000. Depending on the aesthetics and specifications, the price could go up massively. Building a house of your own design would require that you estimate the materials and furniture you would want to have as a single container is sold at $2,500 in the US.

- Sustainability and energy efficiency: a shipping container is a more sustainable way of living. However, this sustainability depends on the material used in the building. The short time it takes in building these two homes causes a reduction in carbon footprint. The smaller space available for building and living helps to ensure the management of resources and enhances sustainability.

- Renovation: container homes can easily be renovated because of their modality, you can easily add one extra container to the main building. However, it would take a lot of stress and money to begin to do the insulation and roofing work for the new addition. Also, getting rid of rust and toxins through recycling can be quite tough. Because the container is tough and can withstand tough weather conditions, it could be disadvantageous to totally tear down. A tiny home can be designed in any style of your choice but it cannot be expanded.

2. How long does container house last?

Most container homes are known to last for a sum of 25 years without any issue at all. Container homes are prone to rust than any other disaster or damage factor, if you can keep rusts at bay, your container can last pretty long. Also, if you wrap it in an external layer, it would stay for a much longer time.

3. What is the estimated cost of building a container home?

The cost of building a container varies according to location and condition. Specifications like size, length, age and structural condition could affect the cost of a container. Depending on these specifications, a container can be gotten between $1,400 to $4,000. Asides from this, the cost of building is also affected by the contraction fee and the cost of acquiring certain furniture or materials. In the united states, it costs about $50-$150 to contract a contractor hourly.

In total estimate, building a large shipping container home could cost about $150,000-$175,000 but if you have some experience in building, you can handle some things yourself and get the cost down by a few thousand dollars. Other none building costs are; delivery, site/foundation structure, permits, and availability of shipping containers.

4. Are shipping container homes waterproof?

Shipping containers do not have the texture to be waterproof, they are only tough enough to be water-resistant. They can take in some amount or degree of water without getting destroyed. They can shield the home from snow, rain and precipitation.

5. Are shipping container homes safe?

   A brand-new container has more assured safety than a used one. That is because you would be getting it directly from the manufacturer or wholesaler. You can ensure that they do not apply hazardous paints or coats on the floor and walls. You might not have the chance to get a container free of chemicals if you purchase second-hand. The way to deal with such a situation is to get a non-breathable flooring underlayment to cover the original floor of the container. Then remove and replace the original flooring.

6. Can shipping container homes withstand a hurricane?

   Container homes are well known and validated for their durability and strength. This enables them to withstand terrible storms or winds up to 100mph. when attached to a very good foundation, their stability toughens up and they can withstand wind of up to 175mph. it is very much safe for places with tough weather conditions or prone to be affected by harsh natural disasters.

7. Can $50,000 and less build a container home for me?

   Of course, yes, with $50,000, you can build a tiny home. However, you might need to do some site work yourself, because the budget might not be enough to pay for all the site work. There are many DIY tasks you could do yourself like painting and interior décor. Also, ensure to get building materials at discount at a fairly cheap rate.

8. How do I join containers together to make my container home?

   Containers can be joined together to make a wider or taller shipping container home. However, this can be done by welding the corner posts, using thin tiny metal sheets, and roofing cement. If making a horizontal expansion, place the second container on the foundation and make it adjacent to the main container. Afterward, weld the corners and bases to the foundation. before putting the roofing cement, install a roofing flashing inside and outside the container. These three attachments will make a strong seal.

9. In what state is building shipping container homes allowed?

United States is one of the leading countries where container homes have become a thing. Almost all states in the US allow for container home building. States like Maryland, Michigan, Minnesota, Maine, Mississippi, Missouri, and Massachusetts are not left behind.

However, you have to check if your city is in support of container homes before you start construction.

Conclusion

Shipping container is much more than just a pack of metals. With the right information and a proper guide, you can use shipping containers in building magnificent structures of various kinds. It is a more eco-friendly way of building and establishing a housing structure. Although, its small size could pose a challenge and could be difficult to contain a large family or more than three to five people, with the tips listed here you will be able to manage the small space and make a meaningful living from it. In the shipping container home, every space is useful.

The selection of a shipping container is just as important as the construction process. You have to be careful to select a container that is in a good condition and fits your designed budget. Also, your selection includes your delivery means. Various means of ordering and delivering a container have been discussed in this book. You can begin to try them out. Remember to conduct a thorough inspection.

Constructing a shipping container home is much easier with the help of a contractor. Their counsels can help you avoid certain mistakes most homeowners make at the early stage of their building. With the right knowledge on shipping home construction, you get to save yourself extra money and stress that could frustrate your building.

Now you can go ahead and order that shipping container and make your container home a crème de la crème.

www.ingramcontent.com/pod-product-compliance
Lightning Source LLC
Chambersburg PA
CBHW071414070526
44578CB00003B/576